1976

kept

SOCIAL GERONTOLOGY

SOCIAL GERONTOLOGY

Marvin R. Koller

KENT STATE UNIVERSITY

RANDOM HOUSE

NEW YORK

4 6 8 9 7 5 3

 Published in New York by Random House, Inc., and simultaneously in Toronto, Canada, by Random House of Canada Limited.

Library of Congress Catalog Card Number: 68-13361

Manufactured in the United States of America
by The Haddon Craftsmen, Inc.,
Scranton, Pa.

DESIGN BY VINCENT TORRE

TO THE MEMORY OF

Mrs. Charles Savage,

who knew how to fulfill life

PREFACE

The literature in social gerontology is voluminous. Although there is no short cut to scholarship, this brief presentation represents a distillation of much of the past and present productivity in this new and challenging multifaceted specialization. It was written for both undergraduate and graduate students who wish to absorb some of its key ideas and to sense its significance in their professional lives.

However, the readership of this publication should be extended to the intelligent and knowledge-seeking general public. The topic of aging touches every life, every home, and every relationship. The material contained herein can be examined with profit, especially by the mature who have "climbed the hills" and can see spread before them the "vistas of time" whence they came and to which they will return.

MARVIN R. KOLLER

CONTENTS

SOCIAL GERONTOLOGY

CHAPTER *ONE*

The Emergence of Social Gerontology

Gerontology is the scientific study of aging. As such, it is an area of inquiry that differs markedly from geriatrics, which involves the application of gerontological knowledge. As in many other fields, the division of labor between analytical scientists and applied scientists may be more academic when gerontologists move beyond their investigations and become practicing geriatricians. In applied fields such as psychiatry, nursing, and social work, there is growing recognition that practical help, therapy, and well-developed social organizations are sorely needed in the face of rising caseloads of aged persons. Constructive help from almost any source is welcomed. Meritorious and demanding as human needs are, however, action programs to ameliorate the living conditions of elders await verified, valid data.

It is to achieve at least this fundamental task—to uncover and accumulate all pertinent data concerning aging and the aged—that gerontologists devote most of their talents and energies. Thereafter, it is true, come the additional tedious sifting and puzzling systematization of empirical data to advance sound gerontological theory.[1] Prediction is a long-range goal of any science, including, of course, the emerging field of gerontology, and gerontologists may someday predict aging behavior and age-related phenomena within specified limits with considerable confidence.

Gerontology is subdivided into physical and social branches.

The former is the normal province of research biologists and clinical specialists. The latter is the specialized area in which psychologically oriented scholars and social scientists labor. This text will concern itself, essentially, with *social gerontology*, defined as the study of the impact of aging upon individuals and society and the subsequent reactions of individuals and society to aging.

Aging as a Process

Because aging is the central concern of gerontologists, there is need to clarify this somewhat elusive process. Laymen most frequently define aging according to chronological categories. Age bracketing in terms of numbers of years of life appears to be part and parcel of folk culture. In contemporary America, at least, the mid-sixties appears to be the most commonly used cutoff point to distinguish between those who are "young" and those who are "old."

The rather arbitrary selection of age sixty-five to delineate "the young" and "the old" had its practical origin in the legislative need to determine precisely when individuals become eligible for specified benefits such as social security. Private plans for the orderly retirement of older employees apparently took their cue from the federal system and fixed sixty-five as the exact age at which individuals should be removed from their work place. In a number of careers, however, retirement is self-imposed or set by the nature of the requirements; for example, age thirty or forty for professional athletes and jet pilots.

In recent years, there has been growing dissatisfaction with the mid-sixties as the demarcation point between youth and old age, and various earlier ages have been urged as the new boundary. Widows, for instance, under periodic refinements of social security provisions, have become eligible for benefits at age sixty. Executive and professional personnel, on the other hand, have favored a more flexible arrangement in which the seventies and eighties become the upper limits for active service. Each effort has had a rationale reflecting the circumstances and attitudes of persons in their "productive" years.

In general, gerontologists have advanced a perspective on aging beyond that of special interests or economic rewards; they view aging more objectively in terms of "process." This gerontological approach appraises aging as a lifelong process in which all living creatures involuntarily participate. From conception to death, aging is ongoing and operative. Aging, thus, is not reserved for the feeble, "the hoary heads," the senile, "the senior citizens," "the golden-agers," or the balding, but is shared by infants, preadolescents, adolescents, youth, and "the mature." When and if this viewpoint prevails, those who have remained aloof and alienated from older persons may recognize their close association with the elderly and take a keener interest in their well-being.

Gerontologically speaking, then, aging occupies the total life span and does not occur as the final phase of life. An infant is nine months *old* at delivery and reaches his *first* birthday when he is almost two years old. At the other end of the age scale, men appear notorious in their scramblings to be death denying or death defying.[2]

Aging is truly synonymous with life. To many, however, aging appears attractive only in its early stages. How much sentiment is expended over infants, in whom growth, enlargement, and refinement take precedence over any losses! At maturity, gains are more evenly balanced with losses, and attitudes toward this middle phase are evident in more restrained or token appreciation. At senescence, however, losses finally get the upper hand, and decline and oblivion are close at hand. Attitudes toward this terminal phase of life tend to be more negative than positive.

Youth-oriented Americans seem to desire longevity, but appear to be in no hurry to encounter "old age." A popular witticism notes that Americans admire aging only in bottles. A more sober observation would be to take into account the deep concern and elaborate programs Americans have promoted and financed in behalf of those in their final years. The announced ideal of respect for the dignity and worth of human beings, no matter what their phase of life, presses for fulfillment. Continuing efforts "to bring life to the years" have brought increasing demands for valid information concerning aging and the aged. It is at this point that social gerontology has made a most auspicious entrance as a scientific specialization.

Visibility of the Aged

Aging and the aged are not subjects that have come under observation only in recent years. Aristotle weighed arguments concerning which period of life was "prime" and settled upon thirty to thirty-five for the body and about forty-nine for the mind. Plato examined the problem of who should be the guardians of the republic and obviously favored elders over youth. And Cicero brilliantly portrayed the status of old age as the most advantaged position to achieve.[3]

In numerous preliterate societies, old age brings special privileges and honors. In the rural America of the past, there was veneration of older persons who continued to be useful on the farm. Even the Supreme Deity is visualized anthropomorphically as a venerable old man on a heavenly throne in the mind's eye of many pious persons who have difficulty conceptualizing such abstractions as omnipotence, omnipresence, and omniscience.

Changing technology, however, has eroded the relatively secure and honored position of the elderly, who, few in number, had been the guardians of important knowledge and functional in social systems. Mechanization, new and more powerful sources of energy, industrialization, urbanization, and specialization displaced the elderly whose knowledge and services became superannuated or obsolete. Even more significant was the irony implicit in the multitude of older persons who were able to survive physically by the very forces that crippled them socially.

Older persons, that is, those sixty-five and older, have increased in both absolute and proportionate numbers to the present 19 million, or approximately 10 percent of the total population, in the United States. Every day, an additional thousand citizens pass their sixty-fifth birthday, that magical milestone that formally stamps them as officially "old." The longevity of millions of Americans is becoming even more remarkable; about 10,000 Americans living today have reached or surpassed the century mark in their lives.

The formerly "invisible" aged are no longer concentrated down on the farm or hidden away in a county home out in the countryside. Instead, they are "visible" in self-contained communities in which young people may visit only by invitation, in high-rise apartments in busy cities, in hundreds of activity centers developed exclusively for their needs, in a proliferation of private and public programs, in mass media, and in one's own family. They are both seen and heard because they represent a potentially powerful political force to which sensitive politicians and statesmen are carefully attuned. Older persons find their causes championed and their demands seconded by "middle-aged" persons who realistically anticipate the not-too-distant day when they, too, will be officially declared "aged." The potential political influence of the aged, too, makes aging and the aged a formidable social segment not to be regarded lightly.

The desire for longevity, rejuvenation, or infinite vigor was dramatized by Ponce de Leon's search for the proverbial fountain of youth. In a sense, this ancient will-o'-the-wisp has become a reality in the lengthening of the human life span. The biblical proof of divine blessing was the lifetime that extended "three score and ten," or, twice blessed, "by reason of strength" to "four score." These ages of seventy and eighty have already been reached by thousands of men and women because modern knowledge has permitted them to experience almost optimum conditions. What has happened, of course, has not been the extension of Homo sapiens' life itself, but rather the establishment of such favorable conditions as better nutrition, control of childhood diseases, improved sanitation, and reduction of hazards and drains on human energy, thus permitting individuals to realize their fuller potential. This accomplishment amounts to what Clark Tibbitts, one of America's leading gerontologists, has repeatedly called an achievement of our times.[4]

But blessings and achievements bring new dilemmas. The survival of millions of persons into advanced years poses the problems of using this new time intelligently and constructively. Unfortunately, the successful passage through biological handicaps and decrements has only led many older individuals into the bleakness of empty time, rocking chairs, loneliness, and attempts to separate them from the rest of society.

It was in opposition to this isolation and sterility of existence that scientists were spurred to bring their talents to bear upon the problems of the aged. Vladimir Korenchevsky, the great Russian-born biologist often called the father of gerontology, is said to have been appalled by the human wastage he first observed in 1906 in a Moscow infirmary. The rest of his life was devoted to research and scholarly organizations to increase the fund of knowledge concerning aging and its results. From similar reactions, scientists from a variety of disciplines have combined their studies to develop the rapidly growing field now identified as social gerontology.

Brief History of Social Gerontology

Among the earliest efforts to organize scattered studies and theoretical speculations on aging was a volume on senescence by G. Stanley Hall in 1923, a follow-up of a previous work on adolescence. In the early 1930s, Walter R. Miles and his associates developed what is known as the Stanford Later Maturity Project to investigate aging systematically from a psychological point of view. Edmund V. Cowdry published a first report of this and ensuing studies in 1939 under the title *Problems of Ageing*.[5] In the same year, Korenchevsky, then a British citizen, led the way toward interdisciplinary organization by establishing the British branch of an international club for research on aging.

In the 1940s, publication and formal organization accelerated. Leo Simmons produced a pioneering study of aging in more than seventy preliterate societies, *The Role of the Aged in Primitive Societies*, in 1945.[6] The American Psychological Association created the Division of Later Maturity and Old Age in 1946. In the same year, the first issue of the *Journal of Gerontology* appeared. The Social Science Research Council had an active committee on aging, whose work was detailed in Otto Pollack's *Social Adjustment in Old Age* in 1948.[7] By the end of the decade, research on aging was well on the way with Ernest Burgess, Robert Havighurst, and their associates, who constructed refined instruments to measure personal adjustment in old age.[8]

During the 1950s there was a remarkable increase in gerontological research, as well as rapid growth in professional and political machinery to promote the accumulating of gerontological knowledge. The First National Conference on Aging, called in 1950, had eight distinct sections specializing in social, economic, and associated aspects of aging. With more than seventeen nations developing professional societies devoted to gerontology, the International Association of Gerontology was formally organized in 1950 in Liège, Belgium. In ensuing years, a series of international congresses were held in St. Louis, London, Merano, Venice, San Francisco, and Copenhagen.[9] The Seventh International Congress of Gerontology met in 1966 in Vienna.

In 1956, sixteen universities joined to form the Inter-University Training Institute in Social Gerontology and received support in grants from the National Institute of Mental Health and the National Heart Institute for a series of summer institutes to increase the ranks of qualified personnel capable of advanced instruction of graduates and undergraduates. This effort not only provided the necessary grounding in the fundamentals of social gerontology for university specialists but also drew together an impressive fund of gerontological knowledge, which was compiled in three volumes.[10]

The 1960s have been characterized as a period of political activity to make the public more fully aware of the needs of the aged. Notable milestones in what some have called the social gerontological movement in the United States are the White House Conference on Aging; the hearings of the Senate Subcommittee on Aging, led by Patrick McNamara of Michigan; the establishment of the Administration on Aging in the Department of Health, Education, and Welfare; the passage of the controversial Medicare plan under Social Security; and the passage of the Older Americans Act. Somewhat less spectacular, but perhaps more significant, have been the steady accretions of social gerontological knowledge in technical journals, university centers, and state and community associations.

Preparation for Aging

Younger individuals, aside from those entering the professional careers now increasingly available in social gerontology, might be well advised to acquaint themselves with the vast storehouse of knowledge concerning aging and the aged. One fact that seems to come hard to those who turn away from gerontological information is the *irreversibility* of life. If nothing else, it is a maturing experience to cross this threshold of consciousness —to comprehend the idea that one moves along the stream of life and cannot personally return to some earlier, more youthful phase.

Few young people have to be convinced that they should prepare themselves to earn their livelihood. Drifting into some assured occupation is unlikely in the face of the multiple, and often confusing, alternatives confronting modern youngsters. For more and more people, education for a job, career, or position is simply assumed. But education for *all of the life cycle* from birth to death, exclusive of vocation, is a goal out of sight and out of mind for many millions. The domestic war on poverty has revealed the inability of some population segments at the lower socioeconomic levels to move out of the grip of poverty, and all that it implies, without outside help.[11] Many aging middle- and upper-class members can draw upon their own considerable resources—economic, social, moral, and educational—to anticipate future needs. Of course, some of these need no urging, because they habitually operate out of their own initiative and sensibilities. From the preponderance of evidence, however, far too many continue their youth orientation or reliance upon their occupation as their sole concern.

Taking the long look forewarns some to prepare themselves for the possibly lean senior years ahead. Perhaps social gerontologists can eventually gather enough evidence to convince people that certain life styles or life patterns presage the kind of life they will lead in their twilight years. This matter of filling up one's life space is a delicate balance between past, present, and future; each person has the prerogative to determine in which area he will invest heavily and, consequently, which areas can or must be relatively neglected. Social gerontologists do not pretend to have definitive answers. The function of the scientist is not to formulate policy but to serve as an advisory source from which to draw significant data.

Perhaps one of the most important cautions concerning elderly persons offered by social gerontologists is the need for careful distinctions between treating the aged categorically and treating them individually. The findings of much gerontological research are based only upon limited samples and specific cases and may be artifacts of particular techniques or preferred methodology. Aged individuals cover a spectrum of personality types and are as varied as young or middle-aged persons. If this variety does exist, and it is thus far corroborated by empirical research, there is necessary precaution to counsel older persons only when multiple variables are most carefully weighed. In the interim, those factors that unite elderly people as a visible segment of a population continue to be isolated and described by social gerontologists.

Subfields of Social Gerontology

There are at least two contrasting viewpoints from which to appraise the emerging science of social gerontology. One perspective would have social gerontology as simply an appendage to an established field of knowledge such as psychology, sociology, or economics. Thus, a psychologist, a sociologist, or an economist may develop an abiding concern for aging and its concomitants and consequently explore more fully wherever this special interest may lead. The other approach is to enter social gerontology from any gateway but to identify thoroughly one's professional self with all its facets; that is, to become a social gerontologist. The study of aging and its sociopsychological products, after all, cuts across numerous fields of inquiry, and those who attempt to grasp the whole range of its complexities find a challenging phenomenon. Some scientists confine their attention to a particular subfield of social gerontology, whereas others seek to investigate the field as a total system. Whether a generalist or a specialist, each practitioner is aware of the importance of the other in furthering systematic development of this "young" science that deals with "the old."[12]

DEMOGRAPHY OF AGING

The population characteristics of the aged provide the foundations of social gerontology and are the bases for comparison with other segments of society. The size, composition, and locus of various age categories suggest the relative importance attached to older persons. Thus, it is possible to describe the total population in terms of its medial age. Israel, for example, may be typified as a "young" nation, with a median age for the total population of 23.6 years and with more than 75 percent aged 44 years or under at the beginning of 1964. Only 5.5 percent were 65 years of age or older.[13] France, on the other hand, in 1950 had approximately 12 percent of its population 65 years of age or older and has been called an "old" nation.[14] In 1950, only 8 percent of the United States population was sixty-five or older; currently the percentage is estimated at 9 or 10 percent. In these terms, therefore, the United States may be described as a "maturing" nation and, with many other countries continuing industrialization, can observe in France the kind of a nation in terms of age structure that they may become.

Of course, numbers and proportions in a population do not necessarily remain static, and, consequently, increases or decreases may alter the demographic profile of a nation. These changes reflect national circumstances, which, in turn, affect future developments. Fertility, morbidity, mortality, migration, and manpower resources are all consequences of the aging process; and their rate of incidence is reflected in the vigor and resourcefulness of a nation and its place on the international scene. Of particular interest is the "old age dependency ratio," which is the number of persons sixty-five years of age or older for every 100 persons of working age, that is, between fifteen and sixty-four years of age.[15] The ratio represents to some just how much "productive" persons must support the "burden" of their "non-productive" elders.

The variables of age, race, sex, marital status, occupation, income, educational level, housing circumstances, and health help determine which program or policies will be promoted and which will be deactivated, changed, or abandoned. Public policies in education, counseling, rehabilitation, employment, recreation, health and custodial care, housing, and retirement take their cue from demographic data. The extent to which older persons become visible, as enumerated in demographic studies, often determines whether the elderly will be superficially treated or given appropriate status within a population. Private enterprise, too, gears itself to age markets, offering goods and services calculated to appeal to specific age categories. The teen-age market is a notable example, to the joy or chagrin of other generations. Investigation of frauds perpetrated upon older persons, unfortunately, reveals the devious ways in which some entrepreneurs will cheat unsuspecting aged persons.[16] On the other hand, legitimate businesses, such as life insurance companies, keep careful account of demographic shifts to render maximum service.[17]

PSYCHOLOGY OF AGING

In the subfield of psychology of aging, the focus of attention is on the individual, his behavior, attitudes, thought processes, and life situation. Personality variations, aberrations, and relative adequacies are investigated in depth, and subjective states are compared with the objective circumstances. Autopsy reports matched with case histories could yield hypotheses concerning associations between states of health, attitudes, and longevity, but morphological preservation of autopsy specimens may vary with preparative techniques.

Kutner and his associates found many cases of high morale despite poor health in their intensive study of 500 aged.[18] Such cases are in sharp contrast with individuals who, while enjoying comparative good health or minimum physical discomfort, live rather short lives filled with complaints, self-pity, and introversion. Attitudes, self-image, and flexibility are psychological entities that apparently play definitive parts in shaping lives, and the psychologically oriented investigator can bring invaluable insight to an otherwise inexplicable bit of human behavior.

Studies in psychomotor performance, sensory functions, perception, learning capacity, time sense, motivation, and creativity are also the province of the psychologically oriented social gerontologist. Harvey C. Lehman's detailed inquiry into periods of creativity during a lifetime, for example, was summarized in his monumental study *Age and Achievement*.[19] His painstaking research consisted of selecting recognized specialists in various fields of knowledge, skill, and artistry and noting the frequency of their "contributions" and "notable productions." The pattern of their contributions was appraised in terms of their age at the time they produced their best work. Notable was the peaking of important works before their fortieth year. Only in exceptional cases did persons in their sixth decade of life offer significant contributions in their respective discipline. The implication is clear from Lehman's findings that older persons do not "give" as much to their society as their younger counterparts. This study is worthy of more attention and will be treated in greater detail in Chapter Three, where the aging process is discussed.

SOCIOLOGY OF AGING

Closely related to the psychological emphasis upon individuality, uniqueness, and personality among the aged is the work of sociologically oriented scholars, whose studies concentrate on specific social or situational settings. Variations occur throughout life that alter the individual's status or role. Such changes occur in meeting parental obligations, in retiring from work, in coping with reductions in income in the face of rising medical and housing costs, in husbanding declining energy by changing recreational pursuits, in facing loss of friends, and in enduring bereavement. Some of these situations are enforced by society despite personality traits of acceptance and adaptability.

Of course, societies also change, and a society's rate of change, whether rapid or barely perceptible, determines to some extent the treatment and condition of the older segments of its population. In an urban, industrialized, expansive society, elders may encounter resistance from people who are "in a hurry." In a rural, agrarian, tradition-directed society, senior citizens are more likely to be appreciated and honored for their accumulated, and still useful, store of wisdom.[20]

Because society's institutions also shift in structure and function, they too are subject to the scrutiny of sociologically oriented gerontologists. Thus, family, religion, government, education, and the economy are basic institutions that affect the status and roles of the individual as he moves through his life cycle.

Formerly, the family cycle was considered complete when the parental stage had been reached; and, as folk wisdom would have it, the married people lived "happily ever after." In recent years, however, students of the family institution have examined the aging family as well as the traditional childhood-adolescence-courtship-marriage-parenthood cycle. The comparative isolation of the elderly—and, indeed, one of their most embittered and poignant complaints—stems in large measure from an evolving family pattern that has no place for older persons.

Group theory occupies the attention of sociologists and, again, aging and the aged are subsumed in this sociological specialty. Studies of aged groups may vary from small church groups and "golden-age centers" to community, regional, and national programs designed to meet the needs of the aged.[21]

One of the most important theories developed within the situational or sociological subfield of aging is "disengagement," credited to Elaine Cumming, William E. Henry, and their associates.[22] It pulls together an array of studies and data that otherwise might seem unrelated. Essentially, disengagement is the withdrawal of individuals from societal life as well as society's retreat from the aging. Elaine Cumming has indicated that she has had some afterthoughts about the theory and does not consider it fully developed.[23]

In a sense, disengagement reverses the individual's pattern of acquiring a more and more significant status and role within a society. The individual who has enlarged his life space as he matured enters upon a whole new course of action as he begins the sometimes difficult process of disassociation from others. From the perspective of a society, disengagement is imperative for a predictably limited future period: an orderly replacement of functionaries is essential if a society is to remain ongoing.

Sentiments and values, however, confer high priority upon individual worth in Western societies, and disengagement is not necessarily endorsed by aging individuals or by consensus of society. Rather, disengagement is entirely inappropriate for capable individuals, whose talents and skills should not be rejected simply because an arbitrary chronological age has been reached. Despite Lehman's findings of a decline in creativity and other powers, a number of social gerontologists favor "engagement" rather than "disengagement." This group looks forward to fuller use of human resources than is now social policy.

ECONOMICS OF AGING

To many, the economic aspects of aging are close to the center, if not at the heart, of the aging process. Technology has enabled millions to reach senescence in relatively good health, but, at the same time, has pressed many to enter into economic disengagement. Fred Cottrell brilliantly describes the differences between "low energy" and "high energy" societies and how such differences help explain the dilemmas confronting their older citizens.[24] Juanita Kreps' work indicates the close relationship between multiple economic factors and the problems of the aged.[25] Mounting automation is viewed by many as a serious threat to employment, as it often forces an even earlier confrontation with the social implications of aging.[26] These are only a few representative studies of the many investigations, theories, and publications concerning the economics of aging.

In a money economy, the ultimate criterion of "success" or "security" is the amount of money available to meet current or future needs. For the aged, the possible shrinkage of income sources is a disorganizing reality that must be faced. For the larger society, the loss of income among the aged means mounting dependency upon public funds. Neither of these alternatives is inevitable, and economic foresight can do much to avert frantic, stopgap maneuvers calculated to avoid economic chaos.

There are advocates of schemes to pass economic burdens upon generations yet unborn. Others seek to meet economic obligations forthrightly and resolutely because they have already demonstrated considerable acumen in securing an adequate income level and security against economic reversals. Which group will prevail is contingent upon which gains political power to enforce its policies. Regardless of political philosophies, economic laws cannot be ignored, and social gerontologists concerned with the economics of aging have done a masterful job of consolidating their knowledge for all to consider. As in all other specializations, such work continues to accumulate and requires new scholars to refine and implement the data.

POLITICS OF AGING

Closely allied with the economists' examination of the aged are studies by political scientists who endeavor to ascertain the effects of the aged on power structures. The growing number and proportion of the aged introduce the possibility of a new power bloc. There is much speculation about whether the collective wishes of the aged can be learned from ballot boxes. When offices are to be filled and policies determined, there is a flurry of activity to appeal to the aged generally or to specific segments, such as those within a particular region or those under social security plans. The voluminous hearings of congressional subcommittees on such topics as health care among the aged, frauds perpetrated upon the aged, relocation of the elderly, services for the aged, and employment security mirror a political sensitivity at all levels.

At the federal level, the executive branch of the govenment is deeply involved with "senior citizens." The Departments of Agriculture, Commerce, Treasury, Labor, and Health, Education, and Welfare have innumerable bureaus concerning the aged.[27] At the state and local level, commissions and conference boards have been created to serve as liaison between the general public and elected officials on matters pertaining to the needs of the aged and the impact of aging upon the welfare of residents.[28] All these structures and activities produce an abundance of raw data for analysis by the politically oriented.

Politicoeconomic issues related to aging citizens continue to attract pressure groups or lobbies who support pending legislation that, they claim, promotes not only their own interests but the welfare of the total citizenry. Such groups render valuable services in gathering evidence to support their views. Because of the costliness and far-reaching consequences of programs launched in behalf of the elderly, their formulation must be based on the best knowledge available. It is then that the findings and analyses of social gerontologists enter the mainstream of public thinking and the politically oriented gerontologist can trace the transformation of informed public opinion into executive directives or legislation.

RELIGION AND AGING

Aging tends to lead individuals into establishing or affirming a meaning to the passage of time. Aging presses upon the consciousness the realization that this is one process that is irreversible and not subject to human manipulation. To be sure, there can be delay and changes in its rate, but inevitably time takes its toll and life is taken away. Philosophically, individuals begin to see the guidelines they have followed in their lifetime. If religious philosophies or religious organizations have played some part in their life, these may suffice to sustain the aging as they anticipate the termination of their earthly lives. If, however, religion held little appeal or was of minimal value in their estimation, they may revise their former judgments but will likely continue in their habitual patterns to their dying day.

A central issue in this subfield is to determine if religiosity, defined as the intensity of religious belief and practice, increases or decreases with age. David Moberg has summarized the various studies and theories pertaining to this question by weighing the various "dimensions" or differences between overt religious behavior and inner attitudes.[29]

Perhaps in the relation between religion and aging one can find much of the appeal that seems to attract scholars to social gerontology. The young and the middle-aged are not quite in a position to make a life review, but the elderly are. To the older person, the evidence of his accomplishments or failures is complete. Decisions have been made and deeds have been committed with known results. Like the wine in old bottles, life can now be tasted and appreciated. Unfortunately, in some cases, the wine may prove sour.

OTHER SUBFIELDS

Demography, psychology, sociology, economics, politics, and religion do not constitute an exhaustive listing of subfields in social gerontology. There are other specializations, such as social welfare, social medicine, housing, family life, cross-cultural comparisons, recreation, rehabilitation, discrimination, community organization, and the study of voluntary associations. The proliferation or splintering of interests in social gerontology may be deplored by some, but these elaborations are generally welcomed in recognition of the complexities with which gerontologists must grapple.

Summation

Social gerontology is an emerging science that deals with the aging process and its impact upon the individual and his society. To some, the study of aging and the aged is a discouraging, unrewarding, dismal science. To others, however, social gerontology is viewed as being at the graduate level of life and stands in a superior position to energy expenditures that ignore time.

The increasing visibility of the aged in both numbers and proportions in Western societies is simultaneously an achievement of considerable magnitude and a monumental problem. The achievement is the development of improved conditions that enable larger numbers of persons to live longer. The problem is how to cope with additional years of living by filling them with meaningful activities. In less than a generation, social gerontology has been formalized into a distinct body of knowledge with national and international organizations vigorously promoting research and theory to refine the field further. Its various subdivisions cross traditional disciplines, and its unique specializations enhance and enrich human understanding of the life process.

CHAPTER *TWO*

The Demographic Foundation of Aging

The presence of millions of aged citizens, categorically set at sixty-five years of age or older, their visibility in terms of numbers and proportions, their ranks as the destination of the millions currently engaged in productive work, and the multitudes who are directly or indirectly involved in service or support positions for the aged are the fundamental factors underlying the emergence of social gerontology. Perhaps, if one were to trace the philosophical undergirding in human history, concern with the aged is intimately tied to the conviction that human life is precious and that all who possess it should live it with dignity. In today's youth-oriented world, the huge numbers of those in or near maturity can no longer be ignored. A revision in perspective is needed to encompass the total life span, rather than to dwell on the popular fixation upon "the young."

Significance of Population Study

Analyses of demographic categories by age, sex, residence, marital status, income, morbidity, and many other variables provide precise dimensions of a population. By statistical processing, vague notions and suppositions concerning older participants in Western societies are replaced by objective figures and documented hypotheses. Further, population study can bring into sharp focus the specific circumstances under which various levels of a society live. One can learn which members of a population are enjoying whatever material benefits their society can provide and which categories are deprived. From such sources can come informed public opinion and action programs.

Of course, such dimensions mirror past and present positions in life cycles, namely, the moment in time when population units experience infancy, childhood, adolescence, maturity, or advanced age. Taken in chronological sequence, assessments of each period become the moving frames by which investigators can observe population shifts or trends. These trends, in turn, become the bases for projections into the future to determine the problems that may arise and their solutions.

Projections, however, are predicated upon assumptions gleaned from available data. Both dire and optimistic predictions have been set aside by unforeseen events that trigger a whole new set of reactions. For example, population growth is often taken for granted in planning for expansion in educational, medical, or business facilities. But, as Donald Bogue notes in a passage he underlines for emphasis, "*population growth could be reduced to zero within a period as short as 5 years under conditions of acute economic hardship.*"[1] International conflict and thermonuclear attacks described as "overkill" are also possibilities usually dismissed as too devastating to be included in constructive planning for the future.

Population attributes are the result of social conditions and, consequently, are subject to considerable change. A meaningful truism that bears repeating is the observation that men are distinct creatures who bring into being their own environment. Thus, the quantities and qualities meticulously recorded and examined by demographers are distillations from a multiplicity of interrelated forces that exist because men have made them exist. Man can, and will, alter his conditions when the limits of toleration have been reached. The flurry of activity at international, national, and local levels is evidence that the aged population is finally being taken into account in public policies.

For gerontological purposes, reviewing demographic data can (1) reveal statistical dimensions of aging within populations; (2) reflect past and present trends in life cycles; (3) provide the foundations for projections in future decades within known limits; (4) mirror shifting social conditions; and (5) expose latent problems of various age categories remediable by public policy.

Sources of Population Data

Demographers generally must depend upon the availability and accuracy of census counts taken by private or government agencies. In the United States, the Bureau of the Census, for example, is in the central clearing house for population data, and its careful and constant self-examination and self-criticism ensure confidence in its many publications. Nevertheless, despite its monumental efforts in terms of definitions of units of count, research coverage, and cross-checks, the bureau does not claim 100 percent efficiency in meeting its responsibilities.

The United Nations *Demographic Yearbooks* and other specialized publications are helpful compendiums from which to draw global enumerations. However, these sources admit their limitations and prescribe caution in their use. The hundreds of millions of mainland China, for example, were last enumerated in 1953.[2] Only 67 percent of the world's population had been counted at least once at the beginning of 1964.[3] Sixty-one countries containing about 34 percent of the world's population lack a current measure of their numbers. Of these, twenty-seven have out-of-date census figures, which means that the last official count is more than ten years old. A serious gap in basic census enumeration is that some thirty-four countries or territories have never taken a census. Twenty-six of these are located in Africa. Less than half of the African population have experienced a simple head count, and the same is true for Asia. By 1970, if all goes well, elaborate planning will have made amends for the lack of fundamental data.

From a gerontological perspective, the age factor is even more significant than a simple head count. When this component is added, census enumerations become even more difficult to find and more limited or restricted. If categorization is desired by single years, only 74 out of 229 administrative entities have been able to supply the desired information. These units represent only 44 percent of the world's population. By single years, only 8 percent of Africa's population is represented, only 10 percent of South America's, only 47 percent of Europe's, only 50 percent of Asia's, only 78 percent of Oceania's, and only 87 percent of North America's.[4] When such fundamental material is lacking, students of population are forced to rely upon estimates and questionable speculations concerning age as it applies to selected populations in the world. Thus, caution is in order when making summations of global or national conditions. On the other hand, this does not imply that those nations with experience in census enumerations and statistical analyses cannot provide reliable data upon which to base judgments.

Factor Analyses

In essence, the interaction of three basic factors causes dynamic shifts in population characteristics. These are (1) fertility, (2) mortality, and (3) migration. Fertility produces the population, mortality reduces it, and migration alters its characteristics depending upon ages of the immigrants or emigrants.

Each of these factors, in turn, is a composite of the many interrelated conditions that combine to produce a total effect upon a population. Fertility, for instance, is affected by the sex ratio, defined as the number of males per 100 females; by sex differentials in terms of liberties or restrictions placed upon males and females; and by marriage practices, such as early or late marriage, number of possible spouses, and the acceptance or rejection of contraception and abortion. Mortality is tied to health measures such as inoculation, accident prevention, and nutrition, to medical and hospital care, and to age-specific death rates, associated with accumulative morbidity, housing, education, and genetic constitution. Migration reveals attractions and repulsions, political policies, mobility, and internal and external migratory patterns. The components cited are by no means all; they are merely illustrative of the complexities with which demographers deal to determine population profiles.

There is a distinction between fertility and fecundity. Fertility is concerned with actual births and is usually expressed in live-birth rates. These rates are important in making projections of future population levels. Fecundity, on the other hand, refers to the potential reproduction—the birth rate that would be realized if every female delivered all the infants she theoretically could. The closer fertility comes to fecundity, the greater the chances that the age level of a population will be reduced.

By contrast, mortality would act to cut down the number and proportion of the aged and so achieve a more "youthful" population. However, mortality occurs at all age levels. As aging occurs, the chances are that the death rate will increase. Mortality rates for infants and children vary and so do not lead to a more youthful average necessarily. If the mortality rate rises among the young, the population age level is raised. If the mortality rate is low for infants and children, the total population moves toward youthfulness.

The relation between births and deaths determines increase or decrease in a population. An excess of births over deaths is a "natural increase" and leads to an expanding population. When, however, births and deaths balance each other, the result is a stabilized or stationary population. If deaths exceed births, population declines. These overall effects help explain the status of the aged in a population that may or may not "need" them.

Both birth and death rates fluctuate, and the relation between them affects age evaluations. Operating on the assumption that deaths occur chiefly in older age categories, a rising birth rate coupled with a rising death rate could lead to a "young" population. On the same assumption, a rising birth rate and a declining death rate may reduce the degree of "youthfulness" in a population. A report released in June, 1965, indicated that the total population of the United States was relatively young because half of the population was under 28.3 years of age.[5] On the other hand, the older population was growing older, more than half being over 72.6 years of age. Such results derive from a relatively high birth rate over past years and a declining death rate for all age categories.

Immigration, which applies to the foreign-born portion of a population, contributes to the age composition of a population, depending upon the age of the migrants at their arrival. If they were comparatively young, the age level is correspondingly reduced. However, with immigration flow cut down in recent years, the foreign-born population has aged considerably and may only slightly affect the overall age composition of the total population.

Henry Sheldon has made a study of the relative contributions of births, deaths, and immigration to the numbers and proportions of persons age between sixty and eighty-nine during the years 1900 to 1950.[6] He found that the greatest source of the more than 13 million increase in the population sixty to eighty-nine years of age was the increase in the number of births—accounting for 47 percent of the gain. Ranked second was the differential between increasing births and decreasing mortality, which accounted for some 22 percent of the increase. Third was the declining mortality among the foreign-born population, which contributed some 19 percent of the gain. Finally, about 12 percent of the gain could be traced to declining mortality itself. In assessing relative contributions of fertility, mortality, and immigration during these first fifty years of the twentieth century, Sheldon indicates that declining fertility contributed the maximum, declining mortality the minimum, and immigration a middle-ranged quantity.

Population Pyramids

The graphic device of a "population pyramid," which visually subdivides populations into male and female and their respective age categories, provides an effective means to examine internal changes within a population or to contrast different populations at a specific time in their historical development. The triangular form is an assumed "normality" in which the large base of younger age categories is whittled away by mortality until one may see the depleted ranks of the aged at the pinnacle. The pyramidal shape is sharply defined in "younger" populations or emerging nations. A more rectangular form results with "older" or more "developed" nations. Population pyramids for selected nations are shown in Figure 1.

Ghana, Mexico, and Israel are emerging countries, and their population pyramids assume the "normal," triangular forms. However, Japan's configuration manifests some alteration as a result of greater restrictions on younger persons and an increase in the older population levels. France, representing much of Western Europe, takes on a much more rectangular shape. Data from the United States indicate that it, too, is moving toward the time when its population pyramid will be less triangular. The greater the proportion of aged, the more rectangular the figure.

From such analysis, demographers speak of "young" populations, such as those of Ghana and Israel, "mature" populations, such as in the United States, and "old" populations, such as in France. The crude live-birth rates and the crude death rates of these selected countries are ranked from "high" to "low" in Table 1.

A cursory examination of these data would indicate that those areas with a high birth rate also had a high death rate and that those with a low birth rate also had a low death rate, but such a perfect correlation does not exist. France, for instance, ranked

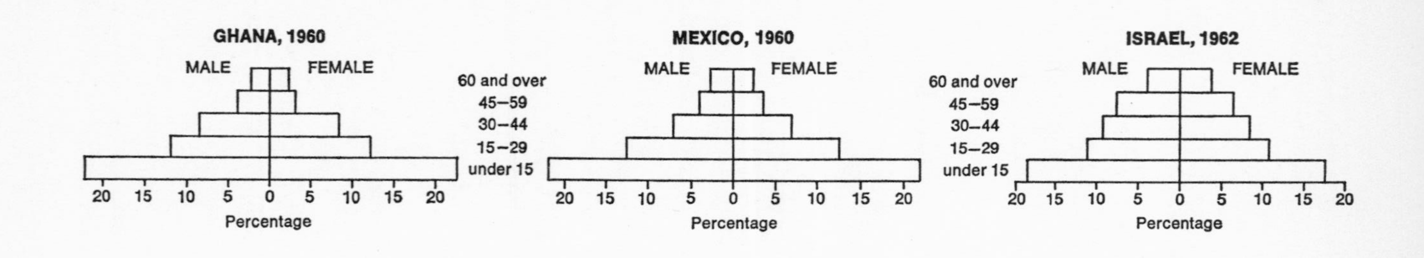

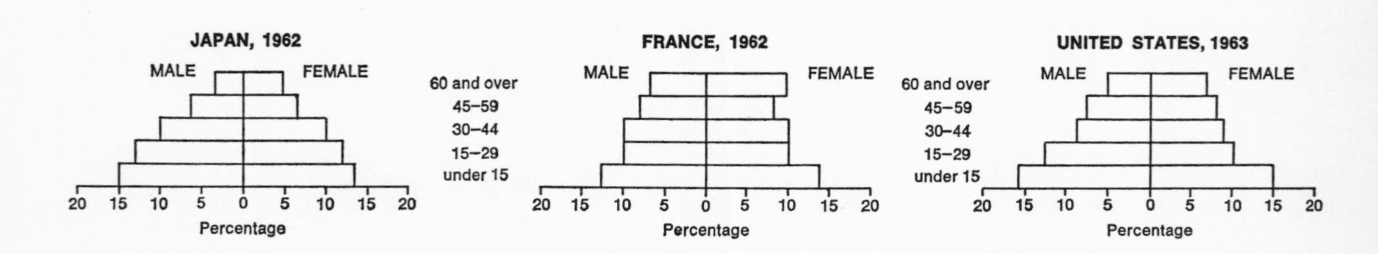

Figure 1. **Population of Selected Nations by Age and Sex.**

Source: Demographic Yearbook, 1963 (New York: United Nations, 1964). Copyright, United Nations, 1964. Reproduced by permission.

fifth out of the selected six nations in live-birth rate, but second in crude death rate. Israel ranked third in live-birth rate but took sixth place in crude death rate. Only the United States held the same place, fourth, in both birth and death rates.

TABLE 1
Crude Live-Birth and Crude Death Rates

Rank	Crude Live-Birth Rate: NATION	Crude Live-Birth Rate: LIVE BIRTHS*	Rank	Crude Death Rate: NATION	Crude Death Rate: DEATHS*
1.	Ghana (1959)	55.2	1.	Ghana (1959)	22.7
2.	Mexico (1963)	45.0	2.	France (1963)	11.7
3.	Israel (1963)	24.6	3.	Mexico (1963)	10.4
4.	United States (1963)	21.6	4.	United States (1963)	9.6
5.	France (1963)	18.2	5.	Japan (1963)	7.0
6.	Japan (1963)	17.2	6.	Israel (1963)	6.2

* Per thousand population.
SOURCE: *Demographic Yearbook, 1963,* 15th ed. (New York: United Nations, 1964), Tables 19 and 23. Copyright, United Nations, 1964. Reproduced by permission.

Life expectancy at birth and at age sixty-five in these countries varies from less than forty years for a newborn child of either sex in the African population of Ghana to seventy-four years for a female infant born in France (see Table 2).

If infancy and the vulnerable younger years can be survived, it appears from such data that persons sixty-five years of age have a good chance to live an additional twelve to fifteen years.

These figures, of course, are not of sufficient depth to suggest what impacts the aging process may have upon the selected populations. Coupled, however, with data on productivity and dependency, the overall statistics take on greater significance to the gerontologist.

It is the "economically active" who will have to shoulder the burden of supporting the very young and the very old. The economically active are those persons of either sex who furnish the supply of labor available for the production of economic goods and services. Table 3 indicates that these persons may, indeed, be in short supply.

TABLE 2

Life Expectancy at Birth and at Age Sixty-five

Nation	AT BIRTH	AT AGE 65
Ghana (1948) (African population)		
Both sexes	38.00	—
Mexico (1956)		
Male	55.14	13.75
Female	57.93	14.00
Israel (1962) (Jewish population)		
Male	70.78	14.30
Female	72.80	15.12
France (1962)		
Male	67.29	12.56
Female	74.14	15.69
United States (1962)		
Male	66.80	12.90
Female	73.40	15.90
Japan (1962)		
Male	66.23	11.55
Female	71.16	14.09

SOURCE: *Demographic Yearbook, 1963,* 15th ed. (New York: United Nations, 1964), Table 26. Copyright, United Nations, 1964. Reproduced by permission.

With less than half of the population in the selected nations defined as economically active, it would appear that the aged, particularly, would be a heavy burden with little promise for the future. Infants and children would at least relieve their "productive" elders in the future.

TABLE 3

Percentage of Economically Active Population

Nation	TOTAL POPULATION	PERCENTAGE ECONOMICALLY ACTIVE
Ghana (1960)	6,726,820	40.5
United States (1960)	179,325,671	39.0
Mexico (1960)	34,923,129	32.4
Israel (1961)	2,179,491	34.5
Japan (1960)	93,347,200	47.1
France (1962)	46,456,260	41.3

SOURCE: *Demographic Yearbook, 1963,* 15th ed. (New York: United Nations, 1964), Table 18. Copyright, United Nations, 1964. Reproduced by permission.

The world supply of energy sources, however, is growing and more than offsets the imbalance between the productive mature and the nonproductive young and old in various populations. Table 4 presents the energy production available in various areas of the world.

TABLE 4
Energy Production in 1962
(in millions of metric tons of coal equivalents)

North America	1,534
Caribbean America	285
Other America	44
Western Europe	573
Middle East	427
Far East	186
Oceania	34
Africa	81

SOURCE: *Statistical Yearbook, 1963* (New York: United Nations, 1964), Table 128. Copyright, United Nations, 1964. Reproduced by permission.

Fred Cottrell brilliantly discusses the position of the aged in what he calls "low energy" and "high energy" societies.[7] He notes, as have many others, that human energy is being rapidly replaced by other forms of energy and that the issue is not so much how to support the aged and the young, but how the productive mature may continue to remain active and so enjoy a high status.

Technological change, of course, has not touched each of the selected populations equally. Some nations are in the "underdeveloped" category. Others are in the "developing" or "developed" classifications. The care of the aged will apparently continue to puzzle societies for some time to come because it is almost axiomatic that social adjustments lag behind technology.

An "index of aging," defined as the ratio of the population sixty years old and over to the population under fifteen years old times 100, yields an objective standard by which to compare selected populations. Table 5 summarizes the data for the six selected nations.

TABLE 5
Index of Aging

Nation	POPULATION UNDER 15 YEARS	POPULATION 60 YEARS AND OVER	INDEX OF AGING*
Ghana (1960)	2,996,140	331,540	11.0
Mexico (1960)	15,452,104	1,939,745	12.5
Israel (1962)	816,760	198,057	24.2
Japan (1962)	27,257,000	8,890,000	32.6
United States (1963)	58,735,000	24,095,000	41.2
France (1962)	12,315,826	8,050,434	65.4

* Index of aging is the ratio of population 60 and over to population under 15 times 100.
SOURCE: *Demographic Yearbook, 1963,* 15th ed. (New York: United Nations, 1964).

The anticipated ratios appear for Ghana and Mexico because these nations have a relatively low index of aging, in striking contrast with the United States and France. Israel and Japan occupy the middle positions in these rankings.

A further refinement is the "dependency ratio," which is defined as the ratio of persons in the "dependent" ages of under twenty and sixty-five and over to persons in the "productive" ages, that is, between twenty and sixty-four. The dependency ratios appear in Table 6.

TABLE 6
Dependency Ratios

Nation	POPULATION UNDER 20 AND 65 AND OVER	POPULATION 20 TO 64	DEPENDENCY RATIO*
Mexico (1960)	21,192,404	13,730,725	154
Ghana (1960)	3,759,780	2,967,040	126
France (1962)	21,187,241	19,960,456	106
Israel (1962)	1,144,381	1,143,834	100
United States (1963)	91,938,000	97,340,000	94
Japan (1962)	42,195,000	52,438,000	80

* Dependency ratio is the ratio of the number of persons in a population under 20 and 65 and over to the number of persons 20 to 64 times 100.
SOURCE: *Demographic Yearbook, 1963,* 15th ed. (New York: United Nations, 1964).

The United States and Japan have dependency ratios of under 100, while Mexico and Ghana are well above 100. Israel alone achieves a balance between its dependent and productive population.

Donald Bogue finds that when these demographic indexes are considered together, the principle emerges "that the dependency ratio in a low fertility–low mortality population is far lower than the dependency ratio in a high fertility–high mortality population because of the reduction in the large dependency load for children."[8] He also notes that the United States will not find the economic burden of supporting older persons as heavy as many have suggested.[9] In other nations, however, this may not be the case.

The Aged in the United States

The precise demographic characteristics of the aged in the United States are not easily ascertained by a layman because the authoritative sources and studies are widely scattered, are constantly in need of updating, have multiple dimensions, and, most important of all, are subject to varying and often conflicting interpretations. Some of the following data provide a demographic foundation upon which to develop some conception of the circumstances under which older persons in the United States actually live.

LOW INCOME OF THE ELDERLY

A comprehensive report issued at the end of 1964 provides documented evidence of the incredibly low income status of the elderly in the United States.[10] Of some 4.18 million unattached individuals aged sixty-five and over in 1962, 63.5 percent had an annual income under $1,500 and 36.8 percent had an annual income under $1,000—or a median income of $1,248.[11] Grouped by heads of families, 6.8 million were age sixty-five and over in 1962. Of these, 47.1 percent had an income under $3,000, 27.1 percent under $2,000, and 6.6 percent under $1,000—or a median income of $3,204.[12]

On August 31, 1962, the Subcommittee on Housing for the Elderly reported to the Senate Special Committee on Aging that incomes of the elderly were low, that income declines as age advances for many who retire from the work force or who are widowed, that income cannot easily be increased because of obsolete skills and age discrimination in employment, and that the elderly have limited liquid assets because most of their savings are tied up in homes and life insurance.[13]

HOUSING IN BLIGHTED CITY CENTERS

Although many older persons live in rural areas, the bulk of the elderly are found in deteriorating city neighborhoods in substandard dwellings, trapped by low incomes as well as by strong ties with familiar surroundings. The Senate subcommittee noted, "If the older persons remain in their original family homes, they are liable to have more space than they can utilize, maintain, or afford."[14]

STRONG FAMILY TIES

The report continues that in 1960, 2.3 million elderly people were living either with their children or with other adult relatives.[15] This does not mean that the older persons necessarily preferred these arrangements, nor does it imply that the middle generation was pleased with the possible double burden of supporting both their parents and their children. On the other hand, research by Marvin B. Sussman and Lee Burchinal on kin networks in urban society affirms that the extended kin system still functions with mutual assistance patterns encompassing several generations.[16] Despite claims to the contrary, filial responsibility continues to exist.

RESIDENTIAL STABILITY

Although it is a well-publicized fact that some older persons have moved into retirement colonies or to the moderate climates of California, Arizona, and Florida, the preponderance of evidence shows that most of the elderly stay in the states in which they have always lived. Iowa, Kansas, Maine, Massachusetts, Minnesota, Missouri, Nebraska, New Hampshire, New York, Oklahoma, Oregon, Pennsylvania, Rhode Island, South Dakota, Vermont, and Wisconsin all surpassed the national average of elderly persons in their populations. Older persons apparently prefer to remain in their home state or at least do not easily remove themselves en masse to "sunshine" states (see Table 7).

TABLE 7
Population Age Sixty-five and Over, 1961

State	POPULATION 65 AND OVER	PERCENTAGE OF TOTAL POPULATION
Alabama	268,000	8.9
Alaska	6,000	2.4
Arizona	97,000	6.8
Arkansas	198,000	11.0
California	1,431,000	8.7
Colorado	162,000	8.8
Connecticut	249,000	9.7
Delaware	37,000	8.0
District of Columbia	72,000	9.3
Florida	597,000	11.4
Georgia	299,000	7.4
Hawaii	31,000	4.7
Idaho	60,000	8.7
Illinois	995,000	9.9
Indiana	452,000	9.6
Iowa	331,000	12.0
Kansas	243,000	11.1
Kentucky	297,000	9.7
Louisiana	248,000	7.6
Maine	108,000	11.0
Maryland	234,000	7.4
Massachusetts	579,000	11.3

(*Table 7 Continued*)

State	POPULATION 65 AND OVER	PERCENTAGE OF TOTAL POPULATION
Michigan	657,000	8.3
Minnesota	363,000	10.5
Mississippi	193,000	8.7
Missouri	509,000	11.8
Montana	66,000	9.4
Nebraska	167,000	11.4
Nevada	19,000	6.0
New Hampshire	69,000	11.2
New Jersey	581,000	9.4
New Mexico	54,000	5.5
New York	1,737,000	10.1
North Carolina	324,000	6.9
North Dakota	59,000	9.3
Ohio	913,000	9.2
Oklahoma	255,000	10.6
Oregon	190,000	10.3
Pennsylvania	1,149,000	10.1
Rhode Island	91,000	10.6
South Carolina	156,000	6.5
South Dakota	73,000	10.4
Tennessee	316,000	8.8
Texas	773,000	7.8
Utah	62,000	6.6
Vermont	44,000	11.3
Virginia	298,000	7.3
Washington	285,000	9.7
West Virginia	175,000	9.7
Wisconsin	412,000	10.2
Wyoming	27,000	7.6
Total	17,013,000	9.3

SOURCE: U.S. Bureau of the Census, *Current Population Reports,* Series P-25 (Washington, D.C.: U.S. Government Printing Office, 1961).

ABUNDANCE OF ELDERLY WOMEN

In February, 1965, the Metropolitan Life Insurance Company issued a report, "The American Woman," confirming the increasing numbers of females in advanced years:

Under age 25, in fact, women are in the minority, reflecting the greater number of males than females born each year. By early adult life, as a result of their better record of survivorship, women outnumber men, and this differential in favor of women increases with advance in age, particularly in later life. At ages 65 and over, there now are 1,276 women per 1,000 men; by 1980, this ratio will be 1,403 per 1,000.[17]

INCREASING WIDOWHOOD

Women are increasingly outliving their husbands, a fact that insurance companies carefully note as determining which spouse generally receives the benefits of policies. The insurance company's report continues:

> Throughout the greater part of adult life, most women live with their husband in a household of their own. Four fifths of the women in the age range 25–44 live in such households. The proportion decreases, however, to three fifths at ages 55–64 and to one third at ages 65 and over. This reduction reflects the increasing incidence of widowhood with advance in age. Most women bereft of their husband either become head of a household, go to live with their children or with related persons, or become lodgers or hotel residents. The proportion of women who head households increases from 11 percent at ages 40–44 to 36 percent at ages 65 and over.[18]

About 12 percent of American men between the ages of 65 and 74 are widowers, and 34 percent are widowers at age 75 or over. Women, however, experience much more loss as time moves along because the corresponding percentage for widowhood at ages 65 to 74 is 44.5 and at age 75 and over, 70.5.[19] These differences are due, in part, to the higher remarriage rate for widowers than for widows, isolating widows even further than the men.

MODERATE INCREASE AHEAD

Projections from available data do not indicate an increase of older persons far beyond the current proportion. The expectation is that the aged will be about 9.5 to 10.5 percent of the total population in 1980. Such projections, of course, are predicated upon the assumption that the birth rate will continue to be fairly high. If the birth rate declines, however, the proportion of aged will make a decided climb.

IMPLICATIONS FOR SOCIAL INSTITUTIONS

The presence of such a large number and proportion of elderly has been felt profoundly in the various social institutions of American society. For example, students of the family system are paying increasing attention to the final stages of family living rather than concentrating, as in the past, on childhood, spouse selection, and early maturity. Political reactions to the elderly are well known. Massive programs ranging from social security to housing, education, rehabilitation, employment, health care, and research are underway. In the 1963 fiscal year alone, the federal government spent some $17 billion for the "senior citizens" sixty-five and over.[20]

Those concerned with the economy have tended to take a longer, perhaps more sober, look at what the expenditure of large funds in behalf of the aged has done or will do to the economic health of individuals and the business world. Some have pointedly noted that overconcentration on the "have-nots" may cause irreparable financial damage to individuals, families, or the society at large. Inevitably, a course of action must be determined, and the pluralistic interests of the people are groping in that direction.

Clergy and laity continue to reexamine what religion has to offer to older persons. In far too many cases, they have found that lip service in terms of "honor" and "respect" for the aged has not been converted to real service and inclusion of the aged. On the other hand, religious organizations have demonstrated leadership in offering housing, hospital care, and nursing facilities.

Perhaps most important of all is the effort of scholars and scientists to gain new knowledge of the aging process and to inform the public of the significance of their findings and deliberations. With such data, the demographic outlines of aging can take clearer and more positive shape.

Summation

The foundation upon which much of social gerontology rests is demographic data concerning the aged. Population characteristics emerge from a host of social conditions and enable men to appraise the work of past and present policies. Unfortunately, despite monumental efforts, census enumerations are incomplete and must be used with considerable caution. However, there is high efficiency and coverage in many cases, and the dynamic factors of fertility, mortality, and migration account for age-specific attributes. Although mortality and migration explain the numbers and proportions of aged persons, fertility apparently plays a larger role.

Comparative studies of emerging nations and developed nations reveal the "youthfulness" of the former and the "maturity" of the latter. The United States population in recent years has manifested "maturity" despite high fertility rates and declining mortality. The fear that the aged will constitute an alarming dependency upon the economically productive is not sustained in the face of improved energy sources and increasing technology.

Within the United States the elderly typically have low incomes with little chance of improvement as they advance in years. In general, older persons cluster in blighted areas of "center" cities, unable or unwilling to make a change. Family ties remain strong, but conflicts between generations are compounded. Residentially stable within the states in which they have spent most of their lives, an increasing number of elderly widows try to make the best of their remaining years. Projections to 1980 indicate that the proportions of persons sixty-five years of age and over will not increase substantially from present levels unless unforeseen events occur.

Such conditions suggest that advancing years have not necessarily brought ease and comfort to "senior citizens." Accordingly, social systems such as the family, the government, religion, education, and the economy have felt the presence of the aged and have reacted to them. Ways and means to alleviate the deprivations visited upon the elderly continue to be debated. Understandable differences of opinion have developed over such matters as providing care for older persons who enjoy an adequate income and who differ markedly from the elderly so frequently described as the "have-nots."

CHAPTER *THREE*

The Aging Process

A guiding tenet among scientists is that there is a prevailing order and harmony beneath apparent disorder or disharmony. This has been the effort of gerontologists in their investigations of the aging process: to uncover the threads that tie seemingly unrelated events together, whether they occur to individuals or to their social systems.

In pursuing this goal, there is always the possibility of following a sterile lead. Among these are chronological age grading, stereotypic judgments, simplification, and overestimation of favored theories.[1]

Counting each year of life or grouping the years in decades is probably the most common approach to the aging process. This procedure has the decided advantages of apparent precision, the establishment of norms for each age category, and the possible anticipation of behavior of those about to enter a new age bracket. Difficulties become evident, however, when individual differences defy age categories, when people simply do not "act their age," when young people are not allowed "to grow up," when older people are pushed aside, or when individual talents, strengths, or disabilities are disregarded.

Generalized half-truths may satisfy some, but the Shakespearean "seventh age"—"sans teeth, sans eyes, sans taste, sans everything"—simply does not describe all aging persons. Nor do the euphemisms "senior citizen" and "golden-ager" distract older persons from the realities of their place in the aging process. Fortunately, a sense of humor is not age-bound, and some older women can jokingly say, "The Old Gray Mare, She Ain't What She Used to Be." But beneath the comic mask, the passage of the years leaves unmistakable imprints.

Biological Aging

The physical body and its functions are basic factors in any assessment of the aging process. So long as the intricate body systems can perform their life-sustaining operations, the individual may continue to maintain his identity and relationships with others. If the vital processes are hindered or arrested, then the individual is removed, to some degree, from mortal life.

Social gerontologists do not normally explore physiological aging in any great depth because this is appropriately the province of medical or biological specialists, who are far better equipped to evaluate these matters. But the many biological changes brought by the passage of time are too much at the heart of the aging process to be summarily dismissed. The usual precaution must be observed that biological aging has been studied by many scientists, by a variety of methods, and with different populations or samples. The findings, methods, and interpretations are not necessarily in agreement. By no means is there consensus that all available data have been collected. Nevertheless, the qualitative changes in tissues, organs, and functions can at least be broadly described.

CELLS

The body undergoes continuous change. Its cells are created, grow, and die, only to be replaced by new and similar or, sometimes, different cells. Some elements in the blood have a life span of approximately three or four days. On the other hand, some cells of the nervous system are said to endure a person's lifetime.[2]

The rate of regeneration of cells is roughly inversely related to aging. Thus, rapid recovery from wounds or injuries is common in the young and declination and relatively slow healing in the aged. Brain cells are particularly vulnerable to losses because apparently there is no replacement when these specialized cells are destroyed.

The major changes in aging cells have been described as "fatty, fibrotic, and pigment degenerations."[3] Fatty deposits, technically called cholesterol, in the cells as well as the invasion of calcium salts into intercellular spaces slowly reduce the flow of blood in the cardiovascular system, producing the deteriorating side effects popularly called hardening of the arteries or, more technically, arteriosclerosis. The heart adapts itself to the decreasing flexibility of the arteries and the increasing strictures in the circulatory system by pumping harder or increasing blood pressure. Trouble develops if the walls of the arteries collapse under pressure or if a blood clot or thrombus breaks loose and denies passage of vital oxygen and nutrients to the cells.

Changes in fibrotic cellular tissue are also concomitants of aging. This is popularly known as "connective tissue" and normally replaces specialized cells. This type of tissue can hold cells together; the scar tissue that forms after healing is an example of such tissue. However, the connective tissue is neither as serviceable nor as versatile as the original specialized cells. Vladimir Korenchevsky noted, "Such repair is somewhat similar to mending holes in precious silk material with hempen thread."[4] In gastronomic matters, fibrotic tissue replacement is recognized in the observation that the flesh of tender young fowl is much more appreciated than that of tough, stringy, old birds.

The development and build-up of pigment granules, said to be metabolic waste products, in the cytoplasm of cells can impair normal cellular operations. Some authorities hold that increasing deposition of pigment granules can lead to cellular death. It should be noted that pigment deposition is not confined exclusively to senile populations. Pigment degeneration is also found among the young, but not in such quantity or with such potential destructiveness.[5]

CARDIOVASCULAR SYSTEM

Life-giving blood is essential to cellular tissue or organic health. Arteries, arterioles, and capillaries carry essential oxygen and nutrients of the blood to every living cell, and veins return the blood for new supplies. The heart, so frequently and erroneously judged to be the seat of emotions, is an efficient four-chambered muscular pump that propels this vital fluid throughout the body. Its steady beating is among the first signs of life, and its flutter and silence usher in death. The only rest it takes during its lifetime is the brief fraction of a second it pauses between rhythmic systolic and diastolic movements of the ventricles and auricles. Heart failure and cardiovascular diseases have been the leading causes of death in the United States for the past twenty years.

Aging takes its toll on the heart by muscular dehydration, pigment degeneration, and shrinkage. Fatty tissue increases, and valves slowly lose efficiency with lessened plasticity and depositions of calcium salts and cholesterol. Nevertheless, the remarkable heart will continue its yeoman service for many years if its owner treats it with the respect it deserves.

CENTRAL NERVOUS SYSTEM

The real "seat of the emotions," or, in modern terms, a combined data-storage and command center, is the brain. This complex organ consists of essentially two parts, the large cerebrum, believed to control consciousness and voluntary behavior, and the cerebellum, believed to be the coordinating center for involuntary muscular activity.

The basic structural unit of the central nervous system is the nerve cell, or neuron. The main cell body radiates an elongated axon and shorter extensions called dendrites. Nervous impulses are passed along the dendrite-axon connections throughout the central nervous system but are found in greatest abundance within the brain itself. Continued use of certain neural pathways leads to habitual behavior patterns, which are not easily broken with advancing age. Age, viewed from this perspective, is the fulfillment of a lifetime's acquisitions.

The most general effect of time upon the brain is a loss of weight or general shrinkage. The maximum weight is believed to be achieved around the second decade of life, and the gradual shrinkage thereafter is quite obvious by about the seventh decade. The shrinkage may be due to loss of fluid, but some authorities relate it to increasing loss of irreplaceable neurons as individuals age. Slight losses lead to such symptoms as forgetfulness or vague discomforts. Major losses lead to senile dementias. Acceleration of the loss of fluid or neurons brings about these symptoms of aging in presenile dementias, which prematurely deprive individuals of their faculties.

REPRODUCTIVE SYSTEM

The male climacteric and the female menopause are syndromes accompanying the aging of the reproductive systems. Such symptoms as decreasing sexual appetite, decreasing fertility, upsets in body temperature, irritability, and general fatigue seem to be shared by both men and women. The climacteric in men is a gradual process, imperceptible until about the mid-twenties, more frequently noticed in the forties and fifties, and rather obvious in the seventies and eighties. Menopause in women is a much more dramatic process, characterized by the cessation of the menses. Normally, menopause takes place in the forties or fifties, although cases have been found in which women have continued menstruation until their seventies. The range of reaction varies from little or no discomfort to great agony as the biochemical makeup adjusts to the inability to reproduce. Some individuals apparently mourn their loss of fertility, whereas others rejoice over the shedding of reproduction burdens.

ENDOCRINE GLANDS

The testes and ovaries are part of a larger system of glands that secrete their specialized hormones throughout the body. It was once believed that revitalization of sexual vigor would restore youth. However, much more significant are the losses in nerve cells or in arterial elasticity. It is, perhaps, in the other endocrine glands—pituitary, thyroid, parathyroid, adrenal, and pancreas—that the secret of maintaining the vitality of the body might be discovered. Unfortunately, research has not revealed that one gland or another is the primary "cause" of the aging process. It is not until advanced age has led to some insufficiency or breakdown in a gland that its contribution to health becomes obvious. These essentially secondary effects increase the physical discomfort of many elderly people, weakening them and rendering them more vulnerable to accident or disease of the brain, heart, or lungs. Accurate diagnoses of hormonal losses and proper therapeutic measures have gone a long way toward reducing side effects to tolerable levels.

COSMETIC CHANGES

Human vanity seems to play a major part in the total aging process. The various morphological or physiological changes in internal organs are sometimes stoically accepted by older persons. But external changes such as the thinning and depigmentation of hair, wrinkles and lines in the skin, and flabbiness are too obvious to be ignored. These changes aggravate some individuals as they age; their mirrors do not lie to them, despite the elaborate assurances of their well-intentioned friends that time has hardly touched them.

There is a multifaceted industry that caters to human vanity in terms of beauty, charm, and physical culture. Those close to older persons frequently report bursts of high morale as attention is paid to personal grooming. Older persons revel in social acceptability just as younger persons do.

The aging process does not seem to erode human egoism and in many cases seems to expand it. Self-assessment, consciously or unconsciously, will prompt some to begrudge the normal wear and tear that has occurred, and others to wear their external appearance with grace and ease.

CANCER

Cancer is a particularly puzzling disease because it consists of the disorderly growth of cells. It attacks all ages and both sexes. It recklessly multiplies and forms tumors that live off host organs. It invades other parts of the body through the blood and lymph channels and ultimately strangles essential organs.

The origins of certain cancerous growths include certain viruses, physical injury, radiation, carcinogenic chemical agents, and hereditary proneness. Much more knowledge of human cancer is needed before it can be eradicated; it remains one of the major medical puzzles of the twentieth century.

Cancer is frequently associated with aging because it attacks the aged more often than the young. Cancer strikes middle-aged females in the fairly accessible regions of the breasts and reproductive system. But, in old age, males suffer its assaults in less accessible portions of the digestive system, the respiratory system, and the skeletal system.

Cancer has been called the disease of old age, but its appearance among the aged is more a product of preserving persons from the ravages of childhood difficulties only to lose them to the ultimate degeneration of biological aging.

Early detection through periodic checkups, surgery, and avoidance of unnecessary risks such as exposure to overdoses of radiation or sunlight would number among the countermeasures. The weight of the evidence suggests that cigarette smoking may cause lung cancer. The cigarette industry, however, does not completely accept this judgment and points to other potential sources such as noxious fumes and air pollution.

SUMMARY OF BIOLOGICAL AGING

The overall physical impact of the aging process appears to be losses, declination of functions, involution or decreases in weight of organs and tissues, desiccation, retrograde movement, and progressive degeneration. The downward course, however, is not uniform in the sense that every organ and every system displays progressive disabilities. Gerontologists commonly note a comparatively "youthful" cardiovascular system, a relatively "middle-aged" muscular or skeletal system, and an "old" digestive system within the same individual. The interlocking systems do affect each other, and failures in one system or cumulative disharmonies between several systems can lead to death.

Failure of the cardiovascular system is the leading cause of death in the United States. A close second is the malignant neoplasm, or cancer. These killers are being intensively pursued by research scientists, but their control and cure lie in the future.

Psychological Aging

Closely allied with biological aging are parallel psychological developments. Because these are individualistic manifestations, they are subject to the usual cautions that there is a wide range of psychological indexes. Psychologically oriented gerontologists continue their difficult task of finding some semblance of order and regularity in the voluminous research and theory on aging.[6]

When objective measurement is made of specific psychological functions, the overall finding is that there are aging decrements or progressive losses. Those individuals who seek assurance that aging will somehow "sit lightly on their brow" find little comfort in the descending curves representing a decline in vision, hearing, taste, smell, muscle strength, and speed of reaction to stimuli. On the other hand, there are psychological strengths that encourage, sustain, and hearten those who are experiencing the incursions of the aging process. These include the gains derived from accumulative experience, such as increased ability in vocabulary, expression, efficiency, and power.

Psychological investigations concerned with learning, intellectual capacity, and skills are not as clear-cut or consistent as allegedly "simpler" physical age decrements. One would surmise that if components were weakened, lost, or altered, the cumulative impact of the aging process would automatically follow a downward spiral. Such is not the case, however, when it comes to adaptive capacities of individuals.

In some instances, biological strengths or weaknesses may be at the root of the difference in measured abilities between old and young subjects. In other instances, psychosocial handicaps or assets may be responsible. The validity of intelligence tests, for example, has been questioned because they tend toward school-oriented topics, speed, motivation, and sensory and perception mechanisms. These measures of ability weigh heavily in favor of younger subjects and discriminate against their less-educated elders.

MEMORY

Memory in particular seems to decline or falter with time. However, there are counterfindings that abilities with data and skills that are in constant use do not deteriorate as rapidly as surmised or do not decline at all. Those who have worked closely with older persons are familiar with their retention of minute details of events, names, places, dates, and seemingly trivial incidents of long ago and their lack of memory of recent events.[7] This unconcern for the present is understandable in terms of the greater value placed upon the past by the old and the usual preoccupation with the present by the young.

The old have emerged from a long history, and the young have yet to develop a "past." To avoid stereotyping elderly persons as backward looking and the young as forward looking, it is important to note that individual differences do not conform to this simplistic summation. Neither young nor old is time-bound; some youngsters sigh over their romanticized versions of the past, and some elders excitedly contemplate a bright future.

Differences over what time has taught lead to perennial clashes between impressionistic youth and age-perceptive oldsters.[8] Some materials mined from the past are worth preserving, of course, because they are serviceable and appropriate. They are the results of hard-won experience and have utility for both the individual and the wider public. Superannuated knowledge, however, retards intellectual growth much in the manner that certain pigments hamper cellular health. As a frame of reference, there is certainly value to antiquated materials. But, in immediate use, they can interfere with mental efficiency.

In a rapidly changing society such as the United States, where change is part and parcel of the ethos, the "wisdom" of elders is often regarded as obsolete. This tendency is in sharp contrast with more stabilized societies, preliterate and literate, that tenaciously guard and preserve their heritage. In such societies, the status of the aged is comparatively high, as they are the knowledgeable guardians of a durable, time-tested system.

In much of contemporary America and Europe, the storage of information is assigned to neither young nor old, but to machines. Data may be retained indefinitely by automated machines that can yield needed information quickly and more efficiently than the human brain. Automation is already operative in certain businesses, industries, and professions, but its full impact has not yet been felt.

What is more pressing to individuals is to choose what to remember and what to disregard. Disconcerting, irrelevant information must be quickly sorted and discarded if individuals are to perform adequately. Thus, it is helpful psychologically to acquire procedures and devices that will clear the way for maximum efficiency. For example, executives soon learn to delegate responsibility in complex organizations. The development of routines that have a built-in advantage of eliminating dependence on memory are further instances of dealing successfully with the details of short-term memory, or retention of the immediate. College students are forewarned to develop "proper study habits," which is another way of saying that mountains of information will not be mastered by haphazard methods. Both young and old must share this problem of acquisition of knowledge, its use, and its shedding if new burdens are to be shouldered.

Successful Aging

Just what constitutes "successful aging"? Two distinct answers have been offered in social gerontological literature. One, labeled the "action" theory, advocates the fullest possible involvement with others. The second is the "disengagement" theory, which promotes removal from the demands of others and the severing of social ties. Robert J. Havighurst has been influential and highly constructive over the years in suggesting a middle ground in which "engagers" and "disengagers" might meet. Havighurst and his associates define successful aging as personal satisfaction with past and present life.[9] In this inner, subjective perspective, Havighurst notes that, psychologically, an individual may age successfully whether he chooses to become active or inactive. The criteria for measurement of successful aging, an internal phenomenon, are kept consistent by operationally locating the aged's inner satisfaction with life's experiences.

A fourth view of successful aging emphasizes the typology of personalities. Some may be well developed and organized, capable of coping with stresses; others may be immature and unable to deal with realities. The former could be called "successful," and the latter could be labeled "less successful" or "unsuccessful."

Suzanne Reichard and her associates intensively analyzed the personality structures of eighty-seven men aged fifty-five to eighty-four in the San Francisco area and emerged with five personality types: the "mature," characterized by realism, flexibility, stability, extroversion, and constructive effort; the "rocking chair" type, who enjoy relaxation, lack ambition, are nonjoining, and are disinterested in work; the "armored," marked by defensiveness, independence, and conventionality; the "angry," generally hostile, projecting defects upon others, especially visible minorities, and embittered about their retirement; and the "self-haters," who despise themselves, are pessimistic, and judge themselves as inferiors.[10]

It could well be that more than one of these personality types were successful in resolving the dilemmas of aging. The "mature" and the "rocking chair" types might both be satisfied with their lot despite the lack of identity in their personality patterns or in their relationships with others.

An even more sophisticated measurement for successful aging has been developed by Richard Williams and Claudine Wirths.[11] Their twelve-point scale measures "autonomy," leaning upon one's self or personal resources, and "dependency," leaning upon others. An added consideration is the stability of the autonomy or dependency in terms of "persistency," the quality of maintaining a life pattern, or "precariousness," which means that the pattern is in danger of collapse. Thus, the more successful aged would be those who are "autonomous-persistent," followed by the "autonomous-precarious." In third place would be the "dependent-persistent," and least successful would be the "dependent-precarious." Each of these four main types can be divided into three subtypes—high, medium, and low—so that finally the twelve-point scale for categories of success emerges. This scale is then applied to those cases that adopted one of six different "life styles" described by the authors: "the world of work," "familism," "living alone," "couplehood," "easing through life with minimal involvement," and "living fully." These are not discrete styles, but rather they merge in various combinations.

Once again, the principle is affirmed that there is no formula or set of rules to follow if one is to "age successfully." There are many paths to take, and one life style is not necessarily superior to the other. Thinking only in terms of dependence or independence, there is little doubt that those who show a childlike dependency upon their society to sustain them are not successful and that those self-propelling, autonomous individuals who give to others easily, who do not drain energy from others, and who, indeed, are vibrant with life are successful. On the other hand, those who can remove themselves realistically and gracefully from others without causing further concern are also successful in coping with the aging process.

One other observation should be made. It should be clear that a life style has been developing throughout an individual's lifetime. "Life style" does not refer exclusively to persons in their terminal years. It has broader significance because individuals throughout their lives are building a unique life style that will either serve them well as they age or lead to personal anguish and regret as well as impose a burden upon close associates. Similar to the physical laws of inertia, there seem to be rare instances in life histories in which persons have reversed their life pattern or sharply altered their style of living because they perceived the outcome. Most persons appear to adopt some style or characteristic life organization, which remains with them as they age. It bears repeating at this juncture that young persons have much to gain if they identify themselves, as early as possible, with a gerontological, long-range perspective, rather than a restrictive, myopic, generation span.

Sociological Aging

The aging process not only has biological and psychological repercussions but is intimately associated with a third dimension—how close an individual is to his social milieu, the world of similarly socialized others. When quite young individuals have not yet contributed to the supportative, life-sustaining system into which they were born, their links with others are rather tenuous and their social ties are the responsibility of older persons. But aging sociologically—that is, acquiring increasing knowledge about their social world—they begin to produce, to widen their influence, to make contributions to society, and to build upon the past.

A pioneering study by the dedicated scholar Harvey Lehman

helps illuminate the sociological attributes of aging. His painstaking work, extending over thirty years, is brought together in the classic *Age and Achievement.*[12] By careful examination of the major and minor contributions in the lifetime of scientists, artists, philosophers, inventors, and writers in a host of fields, Lehman attempted to locate the patterns of achievement in relation to age. The "contributions" or "achievements" were not the personal judgments of Lehman, but were the consensus of peers, associates, panels of experts, and public approval of the individuals' meritorious productions.

The productivity and accomplishments of the selected specialists were charted on linear graphs, in which the overall patterns of high and low productivity as well as sustained productivity could be noted. The periods of greatest productivity are summarized for the various specializations in Table 8.

TABLE 8
Age When Superior Contributions or Productivity Occurred

Field	AGE
Physical sciences, mathematics, and inventions	
Chemistry	26–30
Mathematics	30–34
Physics	30–34
Electronics	30–34
Practical inventions	30–34
Surgical techniques	30–39
Geology	30–39
Astronomy	35–39
Biological sciences	
Botany	30–34
Classical descriptions of disease	30–34
Genetics	30–39
Entomology	30–39
Psychology	30–39
Bacteriology	35–39
Physiology	35–39
Pathology	35–39
Medical discoveries	35–39

Music	
Instrumental selections	25–29
Vocal solos	30–34
Symphonies	30–34
Chamber music	35–39
Orchestral music	35–39
Grand opera	35–39
Cantatas	40–44
Light opera and musical comedy	40–44
Literature	
German composers of noteworthy lyrics and ballads	22–26
Odes	24–28
Elegies	25–29
Pastoral poetry	25–29
Narrative poetry	25–29
Sonnets	26–31
Lyric poetry	26–31
Satiric poetry	30–34
Short stories	30–34
Hymns or religious poetry	32–36
Comedies	32–36
Tragedies	34–38
"Most influential books"	35–39
Hymns by women	36–38
Novels	40–44
"Best books"	40–44
"Best sellers"	40–44
Miscellaneous prose writings	41–45
Philosophy, education, economics, and political science	
Logic	35–39
Ethics	35–39
Aesthetics	35–39
General philosophy	35–39
Social philosophy	36–44
Metaphysics	40–44
Contributions to educational theory and practice	35–39
Contributions to economics and political science	30–39
Painting, sculpture, and architecture	
Oil paintings	32–36
American sculpture	35–39

(*Table 8 Continued*)

Field	AGE
Modern architecture	40–44
Oil paintings by contemporary artists	40–44
Athletics	
Professional football players	22–26
Professional prizefighters	25–26
Professional ice hockey players	26
Professional baseball players	27–28
Professional tennis players	25–29
Automobile racers	26–30
Leading contestants at chess	29–33
Professional golfers	31–36
Breakers of world billiards records	31–36
Winners of important bowling championships	31–36
Political leadership	
Presidents of American colleges and universities	50–54
Presidents of the United States, prior to Truman	55–59
U.S. ambassadors to foreign countries, 1875–1900	60–64
U.S. Senators in 1925	60–64
Men in charge of U.S. Army, 1925–1945	60–64
Justices of the U.S. Supreme Court, 1900–1925	70–74
Speakers of the U.S. House of Representatives, 1900–1940	70–74
Popes	82–92
Income	
Movie actors, "Best money makers"	30–34
Movie actresses, "Best money makers"	23–27
"Best" movie directors	35–39
Receivers of earned annual incomes of $50,000 or more	60–64
Outstanding commercial and industrial leaders	65–69
Receivers of annual incomes of $1 million or more	80–89

SOURCE: Harvey C. Lehman, *Age and Achievement* (Princeton, N.J.: Princeton University Press, © 1953, pp. 324–327 *passim*). Copyright by the American Philosophical Society.

Apparent in Lehman's data are the superior performances by those in their thirties and forties. Notable exceptions occurred in the case of physical proficiency, where athletic greatness was tied to the mid-twenties, or at the other extreme, in political leadership or income level, where the "heights" were reached in the fifties, sixties, and seventies. None of these data contradict the findings that in many cases there were precocious geniuses and many individuals who sustained their contributions over their lifetime.

Wayne Dennis offers a valuable study, building on Lehman's work. It is his contention that the differences between his and Lehman's findings lie in the methodology. It is his view "that no valid statements can be made concerning age and productivity except from longitudinal data involving no drop-outs due to death."[13] He summarizes his study as follows:

Data have been presented from documentary sources showing trends with age in the productivity of 738 persons, each of whom lived to age 79 or beyond. These men were engaged in 16 areas of work which were classified in three major groups as scholarship, the sciences, and the arts.

It was found that, in many groups, the decade of the 20's was the least productive period. However, persons in the arts produced a larger part of their lifetime output in this decade than did scholars and scientists. Relatively speaking, persons in the fine arts and in literature were more productive in the 20's and the 30's than were the scholars and scientists. The highest rate of output, in the case of nearly all groups, was reached in the 40's or soon thereafter. From age 40 onwards the output of scholars suffered little decrement. After age 60 the productivity of scientists decreased appreciably and the output of persons in art, music, and literature dropped even more than did that of scientists. This brief summary, however, does not do justice to the differences which occur in each major category.

The interpretation proposed is that the output curve of the arts rises earlier and declines earlier and more severely because productivity in the arts depends primarily upon individual creativity. Scholars and scientists require a greater period of training and a greater accumulation of experience and of data than do artists. The use of accumulated data and the possibility of receiving assistance from others permit the scholar and scientist to make contributions in their later years than do those in art, music, and literature.[14]

Such studies indicate that certain individuals leave "monuments" to their name by their considerable contributions to humanity. This is not the lot of ordinary men and women, but rather is associated with the "select." Time alone is not the factor that brought "the select" fame and fortune, but time is involved when the heavy weight of evidence supports the repeated observations that there are periods of high, low, sustained, and declining productivity. The continued study of the aging process as it affects the nature of human society will make a bit clearer the talents and the opportunities that exist for young and old alike to use these talents.

Summation

The aging process can be viewed from at least three perspectives —the biological, the psychological, and the sociological. In the first and perhaps most basic view, aging takes its toll by wear and tear or normal use. Man erodes biologically in cellular losses, fatty, fibrotic, and pigment degenerations; in the life-sustaining cardiovascular system, central nervous system, reproductive system, and endocrine glands; and in external appearance. There are clues, however, in the lives of exceptional men that there is no inevitability to biological aging that requires that mankind must continue as in the past.

CHAPTER *FOUR*

Comparative Study of Aging and the Aged

Perception and depth in understanding aging and the aged more fully are gained through comparative studies in time, place, and society. Historical antecedents, economic development, shifting spheres of political influence, and anthropological diversities provide baselines from which to calculate just how "advanced" or "retarded" social gerontological data may be. By examining extensions from the past, by being sensitized to the margins of safety involved in securing food, shelter, and clothing, and by appreciation of cultural variations, students of aging and its products are in a strategic position to evaluate contemporary circumstances.

One would expect to find from comparative study, perhaps, simplicity in the past rather than the puzzling complexity of the present. One would assume that prior events fall into some orderly pattern. One could observe the wide range of behavior associated with aging and the elderly. Contrasting systems or procedures could be distinguished. The flexibility, ingenuity, and adaptability of mankind could be documented. And, best of all, dispassionate observation would lead to the objective stance of the scientist-scholar.

Admirable as these expectations are, they are not easily achieved and do not necessarily flow from comparative studies. Serious limitations are inherent in comparative data and require some measure of skepticism, precaution, and room for the addition of yet undiscovered findings. Reports of the treatment and status of the aged are fragmentary, are subject to distortion or misinterpretation, and frequently reflect the biased or minimal background of the field observer.

Perhaps one of the best sources in comparative study of aging and the aged is Leo W. Simmons' classic work *The Role of the Aged in Primitive Society.*[1] Simmons modestly viewed his work as only a beginning upon which others might build. It is significant, however, that Simmons' study has become the high-water mark rather than a mere beginning in social gerontology. For more than twenty years, the best comparative study of the aged among preliterates has been his painstaking effort. His description of ethnographers as "none too careful in reporting relevant information on the status and treatment of the aged, or in placing it in convenient categories" perhaps explains why definitive study either will emerge in the future or will never occur.[2] Like *Folkways* by William Graham Sumner or *The Polish Peasant* of Thomas and Znaniecki, Simmons' book is a rare monument that few could emulate. Like Simmons and others interested in this specialization, students of aging and the aged have to sift an extensive literature to make out the barest outline of age consciousness in human societies.

A final note of caution before entering upon a more detailed description and analysis of the aged in different cultural settings: be somewhat wary of applying literally bits and pieces from a set of conditions in the distant past to the rather different set in the present. Like the old parlor game of pinning the tail on the donkey, it is hilarious to place tails on unlikely anatomical locales, but it is unfortunate to insist that modern reality stands in dire need of appendages culled from the past when this may not be so.

Historical Treatment of the Aged

The viewpoints of the ancient Hebrews have been selected as an example of the antiquity of gerontological interest, after which the successive influences of Hellenic and Roman traditions will be treated. Thereafter, an examination of aging as it was regarded in medieval Europe and colonial America will provide a historical perspective of current gerontological thought. The Hebraic, Greek, Roman, European, and early American heritages apparently are still operative in modern geriatrics, and their delineation is basic to a comparative study of the aged.

THE ANCIENT HEBREWS

The Hebraic treatment of the aged must be understood against the background of their changing conditions. The earliest recorded period occurred around the fourteenth century before the Common Era, when the Hebrews were desert nomads. Agricultural settlement in family farmsteads did not begin until about the twelfth century B.C.E. in the promised land of Canaan. Their population later expanded into cities, and, finally, the ancient Hebrews established a united kingdom with its chief temple in Jerusalem. By the tenth century B.C.E., the kingdom was divided between Israel and Judah. In succeeding centuries, the two kingdoms fell to their enemies, and the Hebrews were dispersed over the world—the Diaspora. The more recent Ingathering, or return to Zion, has culminated in the State of Israel, which maintains a precarious stability in the face of considerable hostility from its neighbors. "Ancient Hebrews" as used in this text refers mainly to the first two historical periods and to a lesser extent to the latter phases.

The status of the aged is deduced chiefly from the figure of the desert patriarch, who dominated his extended household of wives, concubines, children, sons and their wives and children, slaves, servants, and kinsmen and strangers who attached themselves to his enclave for protection. The comforting presence of many persons under the guardianship of the desert sheik made life more tolerable. Respect for the aged, especially for the patriarch, was essential, based on experience in surviving a forbidding environment. Divided loyalty could and did split households, but the passage of time did little to mar the blind obedience due the elder father. The Biblical tale of the complete submission of young Isaac to his father, Abraham, carrying wood for his own execution and permitting himself to be bound to an altar as a sacrifice is a case in point. The Biblical injunction "Thou shalt rise up before a hoary head and honor the face of the old man" is an explicit directive to the young.[3] "Honor" extended to both sexes, especially the helpmate of the patriarch. Note the clear-cut admonition in Proverbs: "Despise not thy mother when she is old."[4]

It should be observed, however, that the edited Biblical sources are less than explicit in describing the aged and their various statuses. Were "respect" and "honor" also accorded aged slaves and aged camp followers? The Bible is vague on this point because it suffers, like other historical documents, from the attention paid to the powerful and neglect of the powerless.

The baal, master, or husband had considerable power over his household, and aging did not diminish his authority. It was he who was the family priest, guarding the family deities, or teraphim; he who could speak to God Himself or entertain His messengers; he who gave his blessings and bequeathed his properties according to birth order and kinship; he who could decree death by stoning, abandonment, or banishment. Under such conditions, it is understandable why respect was tinged with fear and how envy could stimulate a desire for longevity. Many attach significance to the addendum to the famous directive in the Decalogue "Honor thy Father and thy Mother *that thine own days be long*." Further, it is no coincidence that Jehovah was conceptualized, by those needing a visual image, as an eternally beneficent, but stern, old man whose slightest word could become instant action.

Age was inseparably linked with respect, power, and mysticism among the ancient Hebrews. But there were always those who would defy these idealistic norms if the reward was great enough. There is certainly a deceitful collusion of a mother and a son to delude an aged, blinded, failing patriarch and to cheat another son out of his rightful inheritance in the legend of

Rebekah and Jacob's conspiracy against the unwitting Isaac and Esau.

Long life was viewed as a blessing rather than a burden. Some of the reputed ages of those who received God's special attention were of unsurpassed longevity and require either unquestioning faith or apologetic circumlocutions to explain them. Adam lived to be 930 years old. Seth was 912 at his death. Almost synonymous with old age is Methuselah, who lived to the ripe old age of 969. Noah achieved 950 years. Thereafter, a strange shortening of life seems to have occurred among the desert patriarchs, although their longevity was still phenomenal. Abraham lived to be 175; Isaac, 180. Jacob survived to 147, long enough to see his favorite son, Joseph, rise from captivity to Egyptian leadership, and to prophesy the future of his less worthy sons. Moses, renowned emancipator and lawgiver, survived only until his 120th year, in punishment for his lack of trust in God.

Aging was equated with wisdom, and its symbol was a gray beard. Old men, in fact, were called *Zaken*, a derivative of *Zakan*, meaning "beard." Younger men were less experienced and prone to hasty, ill-conceived decisions. Recall, for example, the failure of Rehoboam, son of Solomon, to follow the sound advice of the elders to act with compassion in the case of Jereboam, who wished to return to Israel in peace. Instead, he heeded the advice of men his own age who counseled a tougher treatment of Jereboam and his followers. This decision led directly to the tragic division of the kingdom and ultimate chaos.

Even if senility deprived the *Zaken* of their hard-earned sagacity, they were still to be respected according to rabbinic teaching. The Talmudic scholars noted that not only the two perfect tablets of the Law were placed in the Ark, but also the broken fragments of the original Law destroyed by Moses when he observed the shocking betrayal by his people as they worshiped the Golden Calf. In this symbolism, the ever-probing Talmudic scholars found a parallel to respect for the aged, even if only the fragments of the once-great talent remained.

Death was explained as the divine punishment for disobedience against a heaven-sent directive in the Garden of Eden. The Hebraic concern for life on earth continues to this day and is summarized in Micah's allegiance to a compassionate deity, "And what doth the Lord require of thee? Only to do justly, and to love mercy, and to walk humbly with thy God."[5] It was not until the writers of the New Testament that the original Hebraic position on death was transmuted to mean a possible chance for eternal life in an ethereal heaven.

AGING IN ANCIENT GREECE

The idealization of the aged and aging was perpetuated in Greece, especially in conservative outlying districts such as Sparta or Thebes.[6] A commonly cited anecdote tells of an elderly man who searched in vain for a seat in a crowded Athenian theater. He was promptly offered the seat of the Spartan ambassador as he approached. The vast audience burst into applause for this gallant act. Respect for the aged, however, was honored more in the breach, especially in Athens, the cosmopolitan center of Hellenic civilization. Public displays of respect or protestations of concern for the well-being of elders were held appropriate. But attitudes in ancient Greece differed sharply from Hebraic conceptions; the Hellenes turned to greater glorification of youth.

J. P. Mahaffy goes to great lengths to explain the lack of courage, truth, compassion, and loyalty among the ancient Greeks.[7] This is contrary to what zealous popularists have long maintained when they urge the perpetuation of Grecian qualities. The cynical figure of Diogenes, carrying a lantern and seeking an honest man in broad daylight, is telling. In urging acceptance of ancient Hellenic values, there may have been an overselling of the Greek standards of chicanery, adulation of joyous youth, and deprecation of old age. These qualities endure in much modern preoccupation with individualism and hedonism.

Although differing from the ancient Hebrews in perception and treatment of the aged and aging, the ancient Greeks were similar with respect to interest in life in the present. They sought to enjoy life to the fullest and mourned its slipping away. Their literature reflected their dread and hatred of old age. Grace, love, health, and attractive physical appearance were rarely seen as attributes of the aged. Men of power could count on losing it to ambitious youth as the passage of the years eroded their capacities. Women could contemplate successive husbands, neglect, or even abandonment. Parents could hope that their children would support them in old age, but this could be accomplished only against great odds. In fact, aging was a fate worse than death to the ancient Greeks. An early death, which freed a lonely Greek from aging's woes, was welcomed as a gift of the gods.

Differing from the Biblical eighty years as the span of life or, at best, the beginning of old age, the ancient Greeks fixed age sixty as the beginning of old age and, consequently, the loss of respected status. A sixty-year-old man was exempt from military service and, in time of war, was even deemed unworthy of being a hostage![8]

Mirroring their adulation of youth, the polytheistic Greeks adored their gods as eternally youthful, vigorous, and the epitome of all the youthful qualities of beauty, strength, wisdom, and lust for life. Zeus, hurling his mighty thunderbolts from Mount Olympus, was bearded but far from decrepit. The Olympic games featured exhibitions of strength, skill, and dexterity in the name of Zeus. Apollo, the sun god, was handsome and inspired poets, musicians, and physicians. Hermes was fleet of foot, and Hercules was synonymous with strength. This pantheon was a sharp departure from the Hebraic conception of an omnipotent elderly Father who demands social justice. The Greek gods and goddesses were age-free superhumans who loved and hated, quarreled, made major mistakes, and thoroughly exploited their beauty and talents. Their models of how to live eternally set standards of conduct and reveal how the ancient Greeks believed life ought to be.

THE ROMAN VIEW

The militaristic, sensual, and grandiose Romans continued the Hellenic deprecation of the aged and aging. Their imitation of Greek traditions extended not only to language, religion, and philosophy, but also to their wavering between an official posture of goodwill toward the aged and a more practical unconcern for those regarded as past their prime. The citizen-soldiers between ages nineteen and forty-seven dominated the Roman ethos. Older and younger citizens were comparatively disadvantaged.

Slavery supported the wealthy patricians, the ambitious politicians, and the crafty generals. Harold W. Johnston notes that Scipio Aemilianus, a successful general, sold 60,000 Carthaginians into slavery. Marius disposed of 140,000 Cimbri and Aemilius Paulus of 150,000 Greeks, and Pompeius and Caesar profited from the sale of over a million Asiatics and Gauls.[9]

Slaves performed menial or petty services, and the *paedagogus* —a personal servant of a boy from a wealthy family—is of special interest. He was usually a trustworthy elderly man who accompanied his charge to school, stayed with him during school hours, and brought him safely home. The original *paedagogus* was thus not a teacher but a moral guardian whom their masters held in fond esteem. This was a rare treatment of the elderly under a suspicious regime that even required visiting strangers to display tokens called *tesserae* to prove a right to food, shelter, and consideration. A modern equivalent might be the contemporary hospitals whose visitors must produce some acceptable card of admittance.

Perhaps one of the best-known sources of the status of the aged in ancient Rome is Cicero's *De Senectute*, in which he expounds upon the advantages of being old through a fictitious Marcus Cato, aged eighty-four, who is being visited in his beautiful villa by two young men, Scipio and Laelius, who are impressed with his cheerful demeanor, clarity of mind, and general good health. Cato rhapsodizes on the joys of aging, such as the fruits of attaining and practicing virtue, the contemplation of a well-spent life in brave deeds and graceful living, increased wisdom, the respect of and opportunity to counsel the young, a melodious voice, and a fearless acceptance of death.

Maria Haynes, however, brilliantly exposes this panegyric through an analysis of Roman comedies played before appreciative audiences.[10] The salient characteristics of the aged glorified by Cicero are treated in opposite terms by the playwrights of Roman comedy. Haynes' thesis is that the vicious, miserly, lecherous, thoughtless, tyrannical old men portrayed on the Roman stage would never have been acceptable to the multitudes unless they were based on a reality that cuts through all sham and pretense. In the writings of Horace and Juvenal, Haynes finds direct statements that support her theme that the idyllic life of the aged, even for the upper classes, was more a fond hope than a fact.

Certainly in the concepts of *pater familias*, *patria potestas*, and *manus*—the head of the family, the power of the father, and the hand of the husband over his wife—there was vested authority in the aged man that could be despised or envied.

A further suspicion that Cicero, and later, Seneca and Pliny, painted an oversolicitous picture of the terminal years of a Roman is supported by evidence in written records that withdrawal from life is preferable to suffering the indignities of physical, mental, and social decay. The retaining of dignity through suicide was an honorable end for many Romans, a view that is periodically upheld to this day. The intolerable situation is resolved by removal of the sufferer. Contemporary gerontologists tend to react by turning their attention to possible removal of an "intolerable situation" rather than of the sufferer.

AGING IN THE MIDDLE AGES[11]

The vacuum of authority created by the decline of Rome was filled by the rise of two spheres of influence, the sacred and the secular—organized Christianity and the feudal landholding system. Of the two, the Roman Church assumed the lion's share of power and consolidated its strength throughout Europe. The aged received, at last, much more official recognition and consideration than they had under Roman and Greek traditions. Christianity softened former Roman harshness for true believers, although the few Jews, atheists, and heretics were subject to cruelties that made the Roman circuses seem gentle by comparison.

Medieval life was essentially agrarian, with certain securities guaranteed to cooperating classes. The typical life span was thirty years, and the truly aged were few in number.

The stereotyped portrait of the humble serf chained to manorial lands does not include the granting of considerable privileges. By staying away from a manor for a year, a serf could gain his freedom. Or he might enter the service of the Church and rise as high as his abilities and opportunities permitted. For the majority, there was the certainty that their lord and his knights would defend them and provide for their old age by giving them a home and the produce of the land from new tenants. A widow could inherit her spouse's property and could pass it on to her youngest heir.

By far the greatest boon to the aged was the solicitude and compassion extended them by the growing body of canon law, backed by an obedient priesthood that commanded considerable wealth. The sincere dedication of the Church to the salvation of souls did not exclude the humble, the poor, the ill, or the aged. Wealth and power were passing acquisitions that should rightfully be shared among the faithful who would soon enter their heavenly abode. Charity, hospitality, and care were essential elements in parish life and comforted many of the aged in their time of need. If the land laws or the family circle could not sustain them, the aged could find solace through the three institutions of the Church—the parish, the monastery, and the hospital.

From its land profits, offerings, and tithes, the parish administration could distribute its largesse to the needy aged. As early as Charlemagne, the income from tithes was subdivided to accommodate the poor, the Church properties, and the priests.

Monasteries regularly provided surplus food from their meals as well as shelter, clothing, and other material aids for elders in distress. A decent Christian burial was guaranteed by an ever-watchful clergy. Finally, under the leadership and urging of the Church, homes for the aged, ill, and handicapped were established. Such hospitals numbered in the hundreds in Europe and provided custodial as well as medical care for older persons.

Although older persons were consciously included in medieval European society, it should not be assumed that their lot was always pleasure and ease. Medieval masters could distinguish between laziness and involuntary inactivity brought on by old age. All were expected to do honest toil as long as they were able. Manpower was scarce in preindustrial, agricultural Europe. Despite the age's preoccupation with celestial rewards, alchemists bent their efforts toward finding a substance that would give men eternal life on earth. Sanitation, especially in large concentrations of population, was almost unknown, and medical knowledge was minimal. The Black Death, which swept Europe in the mid-fourteenth century, reduced the population by almost 50 percent and brought with it the ferment that doomed feudalism.

AGING IN COLONIAL AMERICA

To conclude this brief overview of the historical treatment of the aged, a few observations should be made as the Judeo-Christian traditions, supplemented by Greco-Roman ideas, left a post-feudal Europe and were transplanted in the New World.

The rigors of colonial life demanded strong, healthy adults and tended to exclude the very young, weak, overburdened, and elderly. Male domination continued unabated on the frontiers and farms, in the villages and towns. Women were subordinated by the mores of the time as well as by public declarations, although, "in their proper place," they were the objects of much adulation and frequent protestations of deep concern. Death and suffering were familiar companions for many colonials, and advanced age was, indeed, a rarity.

In the North, Puritan colonials took the ancient Hebrew scriptures seriously, adding, at times, a pious reference to their Christian veneer. Large families, the glorification of work, the need for real "helpmates," suspicion of the unmarried, and patriarchy were some of the characteristics of colonial family life. Widowers would be hard-pressed if they did not quickly find another spouse or a surrogate mother and housekeeper for their children. A widow left with many offspring was a prize catch, not only for her dower rights from her former husband's estate, but also for the many "hands" she could add to lighten the burden of a struggling farmer, artisan, or merchant. Obedient, servile, God-fearing children were living assurance that the advanced years, if they were reached at all, would not be lonely and without material comforts.

There was, however, much relocating of residence. As John Demos notes for Plymouth Colony, "This was particularly hard upon elderly people; their anxiety that they should be properly cared for in their old age is readily apparent in the wills they wrote."[12]

In the South, a growing tradition of gracious living by the upper classes made life less austere than in the Northern colonies. Aristocratic families could easily support and provide for their old folks. At the lower socioeconomic levels, however, aging removed the old from gainful work and placed them in the precarious position of dependency. For the more prosperous plantations, there were physicians, infirmaries, and solicitous care for the aged. The death of a favored slave was marked with a ceremonious burial. An old "granny" would attend a mother in childbirth, or an old slave would help in a sickroom. But these are the optimal conditions; the common lot of the economically depressed fell far short.[13]

The durability or persistence of early American patterns concerning the aged may be observed in the unique customs of contemporary Amish. These religious people have steadfastly held to principles passed along intact from late seventeenth-

and early eighteenth-century Europe and colonial America and that are rooted in ancient Hebraic traditions. Their *Gemeinschaft* mores are in striking contrast with the *Gesellschaft* ways of their neighbors. Their aged can rely upon the younger generations with confidence that their final years will be marked with respect, dignity, and comfort. The *Grossdaadi Haus* on the Amish farm ensures close association with their kin.[14]

PRELITERATE AND PREINDUSTRIAL SOCIETIES

Although Americans seem to be preoccupied with the historical development of their systems, which originated in antiquity in the Mediterranean basin and later diffused through Europe to the New World, they may profitably examine the preliterate and preindustrial societies, which are the traditional concern of anthropologists. In these widely dispersed pockets of humanity, fieldworkers uncover the ingenious means men have developed to satisfy their needs. As in so many other instances, apparent disordered differences fall into systematic patterns of behavior. Focusing only upon aging among preliterates, one finds that the aged are generally few in number and proportion. As Simmons notes, "Nature in the raw has never been very kind to old age in any species."[15] Primitives rarely live to the advanced years of seventy, eighty, or ninety, and only about 7 or 8 percent reach sixty-five.

Perhaps the foremost need of the elderly among preliterates is to secure enough food to sustain their declining energies. When adult status was theirs, the food quest may have been difficult, but not impossible. Aging, however, removes the aged from independence and requires goodwill and subtle or indirect appeals to established communal or kinship standards for a share of the food supply. Generosity is widely admired among Amerinds, and elderly men and women are assured of food whenever a tribal leader hunts. It is a serious breach of etiquette to do otherwise. A hunter gains much esteem if he distributes food that exceeds his immediate needs. In some societies, food taboos redound to the aged because certain portions of the kill are believed harmful if consumed by hunters. The aged eat these "dangerous" portions without fear and simultaneously keep the young psychologically and physically fit.

Simmons cautions against overgeneralization. Certainly the lot of the aged among preliterates is not always one of receiving communal or individual support. In terms of food sharing, gatherers and fishermen are generous to their aged, hunters and herders to a lesser extent; and agrarian peoples are essentially negative in their treatment of the old.[16] As the food quest becomes less precarious, the food needs of the aged will not be of great moment.

Economically, the aged that possess knowledge, magic, skills, medicine, or property such as stock, women, lands, slaves, or a coveted title are in a favorable position. When their feeble hands hold property rights, the aged can bargain for consideration from an otherwise reluctant younger generation. In general, aged men in primitive societies are in an advantageous position where "property" rights are upheld by the prevailing mores.[17] Primitive women, however, are "second-class citizens" in ownership of property and must depend upon other folkways to survive.

In politics and religion, aged primitives in some societies hold almost despotic power; their decisions or whims are promptly implemented despite their physical disabilities. Chieftains, headsmen, shamans, priests, diviners, curers, or counselors are usually old persons; the young have to wait their turn at decision making or advisorship. Here again is an example of social forms effectively shielding the aged against the decrements of advancing years. A social order that confers power and influence upon the elderly regardless of their qualities is the best possible social security the aging can secure. In a larger sense, each age grade, not just the "old," fits a defined slot and is shielded from the adversities of time.

As already noted, *all* aged preliterates are not powerful, revered, or sheltered personalities. Productive labor or service is sustained as long as possible. Each small task performed by the elderly frees the more virile to attend to more essential tasks. At the same time, the "extra" contributions enhance an otherwise austere life. Hunters need to have their kills dressed, their hides processed into clothes or equipment, their arrows straightened and repaired, their firewood gathered, or their children attended—tasks that the aged can still perform. Fishermen rely upon their elders to repair their nets, dry and store their fish, and tend their fires. Gatherers use oldsters to collect roots and berries. According to ancient records, the Incas required elderly people to serve as scarecrows to frighten birds and rodents from their crops.[18]

The elderly can find relief from the weight of the passing years in familial bonds. In polygynous societies, older wives are relieved of various tasks and can select and supervise younger wives. Older men can count on their sons for respectful support, because to neglect the old can bring community scorn or ghostly revenge. In some circumstances, senilicide by next of kin is part of the moral code, but this practice is apparently atypical in primitive familial behavior.[19]

Death is not particularly welcomed by preliterates. Even if life is harsh, primitives seek longevity through prayers and deeds, petitioning deities to bestow some of their durable qualities on mortals. Those who survive into old age are viewed as divinely touched and consequently granted considerable deference.

In preliterate societies where senilicide is practiced, withdrawal of food, warmth, and company is a possible recourse. By abandoning campsites or placing the aged in isolation with a meager food and water supply, death ensues with minimum embarrassment to young and old. Simmons reports its existence in thirty-eight out of seventy-one tribes sampled.[20] Other alternatives are self-destruction, execution for witchcraft or sorcery, live burial, strangulation, and euthanasia. This last alternative is perennially debated and usually rejected as in direct violation of Judeo-Christian ethics.

Selected Segments of Comparative Theory

Simmons hypothesizes that there are "fivefold interests" of the aged:

1. To live as long as possible, or at least until life's satisfactions no longer compensate for its privations, or until the advantages of death seem to outweigh the burdens of life. With few exceptions, life is, indeed, still precious to the old.
2. To get more rest, or, better stated, to get some release from the necessity of wearisome exertion at humdrum tasks and to have protection from too great exposure to physical hazards—opportunities, in short, to safeguard and preserve the waning physical energies. Old people have to hoard their diminished resources.
3. To safeguard or even strengthen any prerogatives acquired in mid-life such as skills, possessions, rights, authority, and prestige. The aged want to hold on to whatever they have. Thus seniority rights are zealously guarded.
4. To remain active participants in the affairs of life in either operational or supervisory roles, any sharing in group interests being preferred to idleness and indifference. "Something to do and nothing to be done" is perhaps the main idea.
5. Finally, to withdraw from life when necessity requires it, as timely, as honorably, and comfortably as possible and with maximal prospects for an attractive hereafter.[21]

Fred Cottrell subdivides societies into " 'low-energy societies' (those in which energy is secured almost entirely from plants and animals, including of course man himself) and 'high-energy societies' (those which make use of other sources)."[22] This distinction enables Cottrell to contrast differences between preindustrial and industrial societies and to conclude that technological changes have produced correlative "social climates" for the aged.

The surplus of energy produced in high-energy societies has had myriad ramifications for such major institutions as the family, church, law, and markets. The centuries-old structures that supported an advantaged status for the aged were either altered or swept away. In brief, the aged were placed in the difficult posture of being dysfunctional or nonfunctional. Cottrell wisely cautions those who seek action programs on behalf of the aged to consider carefully whether or not their proposals have technological effects that could doom their plans from the start.[23] Appeals to the past may provide stimuli to motivate thoughtful programs, but they must take into account the "now" and not the "then." With industrialization, specialization, urbanization, and automation well entrenched, adaptations are mandatory only when and if the interests of older persons are to be considered.

Summation

The aged have received varying treatment throughout recorded history. Comparative study of the ancient Hebrews, Greeks, Romans, medieval Europeans, and colonial Americans does not reveal much progress toward greater respect and influence. Instead, it unveils a tendency to idealize, to honor in the breach, coupled with a need to come to terms with the loss of power with the passage of a lifetime. Although there was considerable care for the aged, action was not forthcoming without community pressure. Fortuitous social structures either granted great power to the aged or left them vulnerable to suffering and neglect.

From the evidence of existing preliterate societies, it would appear that their aged do indeed achieve satisfaction. The preponderance of data points to their relative longevity, ease, influence, and dignified demise. The sketches drawn from the European-American historical record of the treatment of the aged provide a sobering picture of the begrudging reluctance to meet the needs of the elderly. Ancient ideals provide impetus to be morally correct, but pragmatically the interests of the aged may not be in the societal mainstream and so may be devalued. With the advent of high-energy technological societies, however, refinements are required if those who have achieved longevity are to be considered.

CHAPTER *FIVE*

Aging in Western Societies

Comparative studies of the treatment of the aged in societies of the distant past and contemporary primitive societies provide clearer perspectives, but a brief overview of Western societies other than the United States will contribute further clarification and depth. These societies not only share a common heritage but have experienced similar social and economic changes accompanying the technological age. These changes are associated with the Industrial Revolution, which swept away ancient prerogatives and necessitated the revamping of established precedents.

The Industrial Revolution has traditionally been viewed as an upsetting, startling historical development that overwhelmed Western societies. In modern times, its impact is more like that of a vast and powerful river that demands appropriate adjustments by virtue of its immensity. Treatment of the aged in Western societies will occur within a context of industrialization, urbanization, and emphasis on high productivity.

Similarities and Differences

The proliferation of mechanization, factory-based productivity, the concentration of populations to form specialized pools of labor to man the machines, the development of bureaucratic structures to finance, direct, and distribute economic goods and services, the need for efficiency and increased standardization, and the displacement of family-based services have been experienced by Western societies. They share these common points of identification, but not equally. Their dissimilarities lie in the different degrees of industrialization and urbanization they have experienced. In some nations, the ties to the past have never been fully severed and continue in force, albeit altered by industrializing. In others, industrialization has moved speedily ahead. For the latter types, their early entry into industrial organization is in sharp contrast with the relatively delayed entry of the United States into the arena.

From the European experience, Americans can gain some idea of how they might treat the aged as technological changes continue to advance in the decades ahead. Indeed, prior to initiating action programs for improving the status of the aged, American policy makers have turned to Western European nations to survey their successes and failures to explore the feasibility of adapting certain procedures or policies to contemporary American conditions.

Ernest Burgess has indicated why Western European societies stand in sharp contrast with the United States, despite their similar experience with industrialization. These differences must be taken into account if action programs are to be tailored to fit uniquely American circumstances. Burgess notes at least eight differences: (1) the huge land area of the United States in contrast with the countries of Europe, such as France, which is about one-fourteenth the size of the United States; (2) the population density, which in Europe averages 200 per square mile compared with about 60 per square mile in the United States; (3) greater mobility in the United States in terms of residence, travel facilities, occupations, and social class; (4) the American division of political responsibility between federal and state governments, whereas European nations tend to rely upon central governments; (5) the greater cultural diversity in the United States as a result of mass immigration; (6) the stronger historical and traditional ties in Europe; (7)

the lower personal and national income in Europe; and, (8) the American reliance on personal initiative, the family, and voluntary associations, which suggests some suspicion about vesting impersonal bureaucracies or government agencies with powers to satisfy basic needs.[1]

One commonly noted distinction among Europeans is that they are much more concerned with action programs for the aged and the aging. American social gerontologists, on the other hand, tend to be preoccupied with surveys and fundamental research of the aging process. Long experience has apparently taught Europeans to meet the needs of the aged or suffer the consequences of years of neglect. In defense of the American position, the nation has recently begun to pay attention to the growing numbers of the aged and seeks to base its actions on sound theory. Both positions are reasonable, but the Europeans have arrived at their philosophical stance through pragmatic considerations, while the more cautious Americans seem to prefer "pilot" studies and "experimental models" prior to entering upon a wholesale commitment to a program. That each may learn from the other is obvious and has led to international, mutually rewarding exchanges of gerontological studies and programs.

STATISTICAL SIMILARITIES AND DIFFERENCES

When the characteristics of Western societies are translated into statistics, striking similarities among their aging populations become evident. The life expectancy at birth, for example (see Table 9), averages about sixty-six years or more for males and around seventy years or more for females. Sweden and the Netherlands seem to have made the greatest strides in terms of male longevity. Italy appears to be lagging in this respect, but, because of the lack of data for comparable years, this is not conclusive.

The relative "youthfulness" of Canada, with approximately 7 or 8 percent of its population sixty-five years of age or older, is evident against the 9 or 10 percent figure for the United

TABLE 9
Life Expectancy at Birth, by Sex, for Selected Western Societies

Nation	MALE	FEMALE
Canada (1960–1962)	68.35	74.17
France (1963)	67.20	72.83
Italy (1954–1957)	65.75	70.02
Netherlands (1956–1960)	71.40	74.80
Sweden (1962)	71.32	75.39
United Kingdom (1961–1963)	68.00	73.90
United States (1963)	66.60	73.40

SOURCE: *Demographic Yearbook, 1964,* 16th ed. (New York: United Nations, 1965). Copyright, United Nations, 1965. Reproduced by permission.

States, Italy, and the Netherlands and the even higher proportion of those sixty-five years and over in the "older" United Kingdom, Sweden, and France (see Table 10).

A high proportion of population in urban concentrations is fairly common in Western societies, although rural living is still highly valued and preserved. Even in those nations where rurality is relatively high, such as Italy and France, the rural

TABLE 10
Number and Percentage of Population Sixty-five Years and Older for Selected Western Societies

Nation	TOTAL POPULATION	POPULATION 65 AND OLDER	PERCENTAGE OF POPULATION, 65 AND OLDER (ROUNDED)
Canada (1964)	19,237,000	1,468,400	7–8
France (1962)	46,997,700	5,544,164	12–13
Italy (1961)	50,623,569	4,827,070	9–10
Netherlands (1963)	11,965,966	1,061,682	9–10
Sweden (1962)	7,561,588	917,454	12
United Kingdom (1961)	46,104,548	5,496,497	11–12
United States (1961)	192,072,000	17,860,000	9

SOURCE: *Demographic Yearbook, 1964,* 16th ed. (New York: United Nations, 1965). Copyright, United Nations, 1965. Reproduced by permission.

populations are intimately tied to the great cities and their markets. Urban "sprawls," or in British lexicon, "conurbations," dominate the Western scene (see Table 11).

TABLE 11

Percentage of Urban and Rural Population for Selected Western Societies

Nation	URBAN	RURAL
Canada (1961)	69.6	30.4
France (1962)	63.1	36.9
Italy (1961)	47.8	52.2
Netherlands (1960)	88.8	11.2*
Sweden (1960)	72.8	27.2
United Kingdom (1961)	80.0	20.0
United States (1960)	69.9	30.1

* In the Netherlands, villages up to 5,000 population are defined as rural.

SOURCE: *Demographic Yearbook, 1963,* 15th ed. (New York: United Nations, 1964). Copyright, United Nations, 1964. Reproduced by permission.

Western societies are privileged societies in terms of the amount of energy available per capita, although the range varies markedly from society to society (see Table 12). Again, Italy and France lag behind such European nations as Sweden and the United Kingdom and furthest behind Canada and the United States.

TABLE 12

Kilograms of Energy Consumption per Capita for Selected Western Societies, 1964

Nation	KILOGRAMS OF ENERGY CONSUMPTION PER CAPITA
Canada	7,137
France	2,933
Italy	1,659
Netherlands	3,278
Sweden	4,320
United Kingdom	5,079
United States	8,772

SOURCE: *Statistical Yearbook, 1965* (New York: United Nations, 1966). Copyright, United Nations, 1966. Reproduced by permission.

Other indexes of gerontological significance include the ratio of inhabitants to physicians, the daily calorie consumption, and the number of books published each year (see Tables 13, 14, and 15). These "straws in the wind" indicate the supportative aids available to a society's members as they age. The lower the ratio of inhabitants to physicians, the greater the chances for medical attention. Calorie-consumption figures provide some clue to nutrition. The availability of books gives some idea of accessibility of information and stimulation from many minds

TABLE 13
Number of Inhabitants per Physician for Selected Western Societies

Nation	NUMBER OF INHABITANTS PER PHYSICIAN
Canada (1962)	890
France (1963)	870
Italy (1961)	610
Netherlands (1963)	880
Sweden (1963)	960
United Kingdom (1963)	840
United States (1963)	690

SOURCE: *Statistical Yearbook, 1965* (New York: United Nations, 1966). Copyright, United Nations, 1966. Reproduced by permission.

TABLE 14
Calories per Day per Inhabitant for Selected Western Societies

Nation	CALORIES PER DAY PER INHABITANT
Canada (1963–1964)	3,020
France (1957–1959)	2,940
Italy (1963–1964)	2,860
Netherlands (1963–1964)	3,100
Sweden (1964–1965)	2,950
United Kingdom (1963–1964)	3,280
United States (1964)	3,120

SOURCE: *Statistical Yearbook, 1965* (New York: United Nations, 1966). Copyright, United Nations, 1966. Reproduced by permission.

TABLE 15
Books Published per Year, All Titles, for Selected Western Societies

Nation	NUMBER OF BOOKS PUBLISHED
Canada (1964)	3,000
France (1964)	13,479
Italy (1962)	8,797
Netherlands (1964)	10,026
Sweden (1962)	5,633
United Kingdom (1964)	26,123
United States (1964)	28,451

SOURCE: *Statistical Yearbook, 1965* (New York: United Nations, 1966). Copyright, United Nations, 1966. Reproduced by permission.

and sources. The life-expectancy data (see Table 9) closely parallel these indexes, or expressed in other terms, the data suggest the higher standards of living potentially open to older citizens.

The foregoing data sketch, in broad strokes, a picture of the highly industrialized United Kingdom, the home of the Industrial Revolution, the less-industrialized Continental societies of the Netherlands and Sweden, and the semiagricultural France and Italy. Each proffers a special case in its handling of the aged. Each can instruct Americans in their search for "formulas" to include the elderly in the matrix of American society. The Canadian society may also profit, partly from its close European ties and partly because it shares in the American experience of shaping older ideas to newer and less-structured circumstances.

Selected Examples

THE UNITED KINGDOM

The "mother country" not only led the world in factory production but also pioneered in social reforms with far-reaching consequences. Its program of medical care from "womb to tomb" as well as its recognition of social responsibilities are meaningful models for all responsible private and government agencies.

As early as 1897, compensation for work-associated injuries was provided in the United Kingdom. In 1908, the first laws were passed dealing with old age pensions. In 1911, invalidity insurance was established, and, in 1925, old age and survivors insurance was added. Current laws are based upon the national insurance and health service begun in 1946. Critics arose in righteous indignation, but the passage of twenty years has confirmed the wisdom of entering upon such a course. The diverse needs of citizens caught up in technological production were not ignored.

The United States did not begin its program in social insurance until 1935 but since then has reaffirmed its commitment by periodic revisions to provide greater financial security for its aging citizens. Diverse and limited programs predicated upon private initiative and nineteenth-century philosophies simply were not adequate to reach all citizens. For many, the benefits never keep pace with America's inflationary economy. Although there are complaints about bureaucratic decisions or procedures, the consensus is that some national program must be supported.[2] The objective of economic and social consideration for persons of all ages is clear. The focus of the perennial debates in public and private circles is upon the ways and means to achieve that objective.

The healthy state of the population in the United Kingdom is evident in the progressive reduction of its death rate, the rising birth rate, and the increase in life expectancy. Favorable population levels are credited to better nutrition, rising standard of living, advance in medical science, improved health measures, better working conditions, education in personal hygiene, public and private schemes to make health services available to all, and the smaller size of families, which reduces strain on mothers and results in better care for children.[3]

Despite one of the highest population densities in the world (554 persons per square mile in the United Kingdom and 863 per square mile in England alone in 1961), the health of the populace is generally excellent. The infant mortality rate—deaths per thousand live births—in Britain has fallen 80 percent since 1900, and deaths in childbirth are now 8 percent of the 1934 figure.[4]

Mortality has risen for certain population segments because the chronic diseases of middle and old age, such as lung cancer and coronary thrombosis, have not yet been conquered. In mid-1964, the age distribution was estimated to be 23.2 percent for those under fifteen, 65 percent for those in the working-age population between fifteen and sixty-four, and 11.9 percent for persons sixty-five years and older.[5]

The general preference in the United Kingdom appears to be for private housing for persons of all ages, reflecting the characteristic British concern for independence and family privacy. In 1961, 97 percent of the population lived in private households and 1.5 percent in "conglomerate" situations, and only 1.5 percent lived in hospitals or homes for the aged.[6]

But the desire for independence among the British does not imply refusal to receive services and aids from the greater urbanized society. The state is viewed as responsible for supplying a wide range of services—including family allowances; social insurance; help for war victims; financial assistance; health and welfare services for mothers, young children, the sick, the mentally retarded, the elderly and handicapped, and problem families—and for education, employment, and housing services. Public authorities in the United Kingdom are spending in the vicinity of £5.23 billion annually ($14.64 billion) or close to £100 per capita annually for this vast array of services.[7]

A specific goal in the United Kingdom is to permit older persons to live as long as possible in the familiar surroundings of their homes, friends, and relatives. When the aged are unable to perform small domestic tasks such as meal preparation, cleaning, and minor repairs or to afford temporary nursing care, home services are available through local voluntary organizations and are underwritten or supplemented by government services. Local Old People's Welfare Committees work in conjunction with the National Old People's Welfare Council. Such a network of organized services augurs well for the peace of mind of the elderly.

Gerontological research has received much support from the Nuffield Foundation, initiated in 1943 by Lord Nuffield. This foundation established the National Corporation for the Care of Old People, which seeks to stimulate and give financial support to plans in behalf of the aged. These plans include the development of expert technical advisory services as well as research and experimentation. With such agencies lending their tremendous resources to encourage study, experimentation, and organized efforts, social gerontology will attract some of the finest scholars in the land.

A current trend, echoed on the Continent, is to create smaller housing units for the aged rather than large, hospitallike, regimented institutions. Units housing forty to sixty persons seem to be the preferred size. These are not placed in isolated areas but are scattered in urban centers or in locations with urban access, within easy reach of transportation, shopping centers, and recreational facilities.[8]

In all these activities in behalf of the aged, the United Kingdom rates as a pacesetter. Interested persons and organizations in the United States have kept closely in touch with gerontological developments in Britain and seek to adapt parallel activities to American conditions.

SWEDEN

Perhaps the outstanding characteristic of the Swedish approach to the aged is their leadership in the field of housing. They seem conscious of the emotional contagion that accompanies surrender of one's independence. They sense the psychological effects of association with those who are ill or dying in large hospital-oriented institutions. The distinction between the "well-aged" and the "sick-aged," and their respective treatment, is paramount in the Swedish approach to the aged.

In 1947–1948, the National Social Welfare Board, an agency of the Ministry for Social Affairs, Labor, and Housing, activated a parliamentary resolution calling for modernization of homes for the well-aged. Instead of building "poorhouses," "infirmaries," or "county homes," Sweden embarked on a deliberate course to provide attractive and comfortable small-unit housing for its elderly. To be sure, the "homes" they developed represent collectivities of the aged and differ from the homes of the younger population of Sweden. But they are viewed as architectural achievements of considerable value and of particular interest to Americans, who are notably unimaginative in housing. The President's Council on Aging, which was operative in 1962, published an attractive bulletin based upon the Swedish experimental housing for the aged to stimulate interest in this area.[9]

Swedish housing facilities for the elderly are designed to preserve the identity of each resident. Entryways list names; each resident has a separate mail box and often a separate entrance and exit. Corridors are broken by attractive lounge areas. Sills hold flowering plants. Drapery, flooring, and wall décor are tastefully and artistically presented. There is ample window space to catch sunshine and provide pleasing vistas. Personal furniture is allowed in each room or apartment to keep the resident in touch with familiar and cherished associations. Special furniture with higher elevation and sturdy construction features is designed to seat the elderly comfortably.

Each resident is encouraged to be as active as he wishes in the community, is guaranteed privacy and dignity, and lives as a free person so long as he can manage his affairs. The Swedish aphorism "Heaven in this world is to be alone when I want it; Hell is to be alone when I don't want it" apparently is followed wherever and whenever possible.[10]

At age sixty-seven, everyone receives a liberal old age pension free from any contribution or means test. Supplements are granted for children under sixteen, for wives, for deferment of payments for upkeep of property or health, for disabilities, or for housing costs. Perhaps most important, pensions are tied to the cost of living, a feature that is still widely debated in the United States.

The state is viewed not as an ever-watchful father image that dominates, threatens, and requires obeisance. Rather, it represents the free spirit of the Swedish people seeking to encourage, support, and "enable" all citizens. Elderly people are not permitted to sink into economic distress simply because they are no longer as productive as they once were. Or, if they have earned and accumulated wealth, this is not treated as a signal for differential treatment. Rather, the Swedish perspective calls for retaining economic rewards for those who have earned them. It also implies that the less fortunate are appreciated for their past labors and services as well as for their human dignity.

Robert Havighurst has studied the various roles of the Swedish elderly and found their situation admirable, but not necessarily free from tension, conflict, or anxiety.[11] As members of voluntary associations, the Swedish are relatively active. The Swedish Red Cross has special appeal because of its leadership training home-service personnel in behalf of the aged. The Old Age Pensioners Association is supported loyally, but there is some opposition among the elderly who feel that it is too closely aligned with the Social Democrat political party. Participation in voluntary associations, however, declines progressively with advancing years for many. The interest may still be there, but declining energies force a reduction in club affairs.

Travel, politics, religious activities, and craft hobbies have wide appeal for the Swedish aged. The model set by the tennis-playing and venerable King Gustav for his people was an inspirational symbol to continue healthy outdoor activities as long as one can. Perhaps the golfing of former President Eisenhower or the brisk morning walks of former President Truman are parallel models of busy, responsible older gentlemen that can inspire the aging American public.

Where possible, the aged of Sweden remain active economically—a choice that many Western society members make

TABLE 16

Economically Active, Age Sixty-five and Older, for Selected Western Societies

Nation	Total Population		Ages 65 and Older	
	AGE	%	AGE	%
Canada		35.7	65–69	29.5
(1961)	15 and older		70 and older	10.6
France		42.4	65–69	28.4
(1962)	15 and older		70–74	16.0
			75 and older	7.8
Italy		39.7	65–74	15.9
(1961)	10 and older		75 and older	7.5
Netherlands		36.4	65–69	28.8
(1960)	15 and older		70–74	9.4
			75 and older	3.5
Sweden		43.3	65–69	28.8
(1960)	15 and older		70–74	10.8
			75 and older	3.8
United States		39.0	65–69	29.3
(1960)	14 and older		70–74	18.3
			75 and older	9.0

SOURCE: *Demographic Yearbook, 1964,* 16th ed. (New York: United Nations, 1965).

to postpone their entry into the nonproductive ranks (see Table 16).

About 29 percent of those sixty-five to sixty-nine years of age in both Sweden and the United States remained economically active in 1960. After age seventy, the Swedish aged remove themselves from their usual employment at a faster rate than those in the United States. Among the factors to explain the difference would appear to be Sweden's more liberal old-age security program.

The trend in Western societies appears to be the reduction or limitation of the work force by delaying entry of youngsters by prolonged educational training and by earlier retiring of older workers. Apparently, in the United States, the extended educational period for youth is well entrenched, but the pattern of shifting the aged to noneconomic activities has been resisted. If there is truth in the notion that the European experience foreshadows the American experience, then early retirement for older workers will be well established in the near future.

FRANCE

Because of its unique history and semirural traditions, France stands apart from other Western societies. French policy toward the aged is influenced by its concepts of solidarity, family unity, categorical treatment, mutuality, and decentralization. By solidarity, the French mean that every citizen is an integral part of the nation and consequently merits attention to his special needs. Benefits, however, tend to favor family allowances for dependent children; 35 percent of the total benefits paid are in the form of family allowances. This is markedly higher than five other Western European countries, where from 3 to 25 percent of benefits paid are family allowances.[12] This policy is obviously an effort to move away from the low birth rate that has troubled France for many years. Some 35 percent of the social security benefits chiefly go to those families with three or more children, which involves about half of the children in the nation and one-eighth of French families.[13]

While committed to all citizens in need, the French have a variety of categories of specific aid or support that can be given a beneficiary. This is regarded by the French as "more humane" than an "across the board" or "blanket" treatment of the needy and the poor. The French acknowledge, however, that more must be done in the future for large families and for the aged.

By the term "mutuality," the French mean that they favor the removal of the central government from social security schemes, except, perhaps, in a supervisory capacity. Elected administrative councils function at local, regional, and national levels and are viewed as nongovernmental. Mutuality stresses the contractual nature of the system: the economically active population will support the noneconomically active until such time that oncoming generations will remove the current "givers" to the status of "receivers."

The purpose of decentralization, of course, is to remove the paternalism and authoritarianism of a remote and impersonal central government. Technically, authority is vested in representative councils numbering some 122 primary *caisses*, or agencies that deal with social insurance, and 16 related regional *caisses*. For family allowances alone, there are some 114 local *caisses* and one national supervisory *caisse*. More recently, however, the Minister of Labor has been authorized to suspend or nullify various local decisions, an innovation that undermines decentralization and local community independence.

In most Western societies, an obligation to support aging parents has been inherited from the extended family system of the past. France has written this moral obligation into law but obviously is prepared to meet the needs of the indigent aged wherever possible. The United Kingdom, on the other hand, has abolished the formal requirement to render support to parents, but investigators continue to find the old pattern of kinship support and concern.[14] According to a recent study, the kinship network of support continues in the United States as well.[15]

A Quasi Minority Group?

It is the contention of some social gerontologists that wherever one looks, especially in Western societies, the aged are, for all practical purposes, a minority group. Milton Barron notes the trials familiar to minorities when he cites the stereotyping, subordination, prejudice, and discrimination suffered by the aged. Further, he notes the retaliatory efforts on the part of the aged to form pressure groups to secure government support for freedom from "unfair" practices.[16]

There are some noteworthy differences, however, that soften this view. Whereas "majorities" may set "minorities" apart on the basis of differences that they know they can never experience themselves, the same condition does not exist between the young and the old. Inevitably, the status of the elderly will be conferred upon the current young. Further, minority status is usually experienced from earliest childhood. In the case of growing old, minority status is not reached until later maturity. The choice of the term "quasi minority" reflects some hesitancy to sum up categorically the status of the aged in Western societies. It is provocative enough, however, to indicate "near-equivalents" and so may arouse intelligent concern among the informed.

Summation

There is no doubt that Western societies are wrestling with gerontological problems. It would be unrealistic to assume that each one will develop identical formulas to relieve the distress of the aged caught up in an industrialized age. They are all groping for new ways to incorporate the elderly into an industrialized economy and can instruct each other by the pragmatic solutions they attempt with the limited knowledge currently available to them.

Technological change originated in Western European societies and has more recently been felt in the United States. Although quite different from European nations, the American society has much to gain by observing the European programs and philosophies concerned with the aged. Americans appear to be a generation or more behind practical European experimentation programs for the elderly. Americans, however, have the advantage of learning from Europe's mistakes.

CHAPTER *SIX*

Aging and the Individual

One of the most common reactions to gerontological study is that the observers do not "truly know" the observed, namely, the aged. The criticism is that objective, external, dispassionate descriptions and analyses somehow miss their mark because the investigators lack the necessary experience and psychological depth to delve into the subjective, highly personal experience of being "old."

Sidney and Alice Pressey, for instance, note that "almost all the huge literature on that subject is by people who have never been there."[1] Robert Havighurst raised the same issue when he sought to encourage elderly informants to write introspective essays on how it feels to grow old. He asked the question because "In spite of all the remarkable research of the past 40 years in gerontology—biological, sociological, and psychological—one of the major persistent questions has gone unanswered. We do not know how it *feels* to grow old."[2]

In brief, the thesis is advanced that "youth" is a familiar life stage to those studying gerontological phenomena, although perhaps more is forgotten or distorted than is usually admitted, whereas the state of being "old" eludes or defies description from a subjective point of view because most investigators have not yet been there. Although there appears to be no fully acceptable substitute for direct experience, there is no shortage of published data purporting to unveil the nature of aging.

These materials are relevant if they fall into recognizable or repeated patterns. All gerontologists will someday know how it feels to be old and will be in a better position to know why they have landed in a particular portion of a vast spectrum of possibilities. Further, they might be more aware of what factors impelled them to move in the direction they did and what factors deterred them from moving in another. Hopefully, all informed persons will benefit from instructive and perceptive gerontological data that suggest the personal and social control needed to attain desired ends.

One poignant effort to comprehend the psychological feeling-status of the elderly occurred in a Sunday school class of kindergarten children who wanted to "know" how it feels to be "old." An eighty-year-old lady sat in their midst and invited her audience to ask her whatever questions puzzled them about aging. One little boy hesitantly requested permission to come close to her and to feel her facial wrinkles. When she graciously granted his request, he remarked how soft they felt and asked if they "hurt" her in any way. She replied, "No, honey, wrinkles do not hurt on the outside, but they do 'hurt,' just a little, on the inside."

The Variety of Elderly

The task of exploring the inner environment of older persons is complicated by the wide-ranging characteristics of aging individuals. In 1963, for example, the President's Council on Aging prefaced their comprehensive report *The Older American* by observing that:

> The Older American has nearly 18 million faces. The faces are those of:
>
> Three ex-Presidents.
> Nearly ten percent of the entire United States population.
> Nearly 1½ million people living on farms.
> More than one out of four United States Senators.
> Almost 2 million people working full time.
> Two of the nine United States Supreme Court Justices.
> More than 10,000 people over 100 years old.

Over 12½ million people getting social security benefits.
Over 2.3 million war veterans.
More than 3 million people who migrated from Europe to the United States.[3]

All they could present was "a composite picture":

He may be between 65 and 70 but he is probably older. He may have an adequate income but probably not. He may be working but it is unlikely. He may have a high school education but probably doesn't.

He may be in good health but probably isn't. He may not receive social security but probably does. He would like to have more to do but the opportunities do not exist. He may collect a private pension but probably doesn't.

He may have adequate health insurance but probably doesn't. He may live alone but probably not.[4]

To all this might be added the observation "He is probably a she."

Physical Changes

The most fundamental changes that occur to aging individuals are their apparent losses in terms of physiological functions. Most biological investigations of the aging confirm in detail the internal and external declines in organic functioning. These decrements may be summarized as follows:[5]

- *Brain and nervous system:* overall slowness of reaction, possible impairment in initiative, disturbances in thinking and judgment, short-range memory losses or absentmindedness
- *Eyes and vision:* diminishing visual acuity, decreasing light accommodation, poor night vision, difficulty distinguishing blue and green light, falling off lateral vision, receding clarity[6]
- *Ears and hearing:* loss of hearing ability, presbycusis slowly cutting down ability to hear higher pitches, and increasing inability to hear normal ranges[7]

- *Nose and tongue:* suspected losses in olfactory nerves, decreasing taste sensations
- *Teeth:* recession of jaws, gum difficulties, and decay and loss of teeth[8]
- *Voice:* limiting of pitch, less volume, prolongation of sound increasingly difficult, slower speech
- *Heart:* increasing rate of heartbeat, increased blood pressure, declines in total blood flow[9]
- *Lungs:* decreasing ability to transfer oxygen to bloodstream, slower breathing rates
- *Digestive system:* diminishing volume of gastric juices, but fairly stable overall ability to absorb foods for tissue-building
- *Reproductive system:* menopause for women, slower climacteric for men, sexual activity not necessarily impaired
- *Bowels and bladder:* loss of muscle tone, prostate enlargement, increasing urination but less volume of urine, possible constipation
- *Feet:* ligament elasticity reduced, less padding, proneness to bruises and calluses, less sensitivity to temperature changes
- *Skin:* laxness and wrinkles, lighter skin complexions prone to quicker aging

None of these physical changes would present an encouraging picture to those contemplating what the aging process does to the body. However, many of the declining functions are amenable to correction and can be arrested or modified by appropriate health measures. Every individual does not suffer these declines in the same way or at the same rate. Each person brings to his situation his own genetic durability, his health habits, his particular attitudes, and a variety of other factors, all of which predispose him to either accept or rail against nature's changes.

The evidence is overwhelming, however, that illness, disability, and chronic pain correlate highly with increasing age.[10] Because the sick-aged are often hidden away in hospitals or nursing homes, their cases are not before the general public.

For the aged patients and their families, the results are depressing isolation and alienation, psychologically and socially. The feeling-state borders on abandonment, strikingly parallel to the practices of certain preliterate societies of the past.

Attitudes

Just how one views the imperceptible, but measurable, internal changes in organs and their functions as one grows older, and the perhaps ego-shattering changes in physical appearance, depends largely on the set of responses one has acquired through a lifetime. Woodrow Morris is one of many gerontologists who caution against forming attitudes in youth that are essentially incompatible with aging.[11]

If an individual has succumbed to the barrage of stimuli that glorify youthfulness, then it follows that when that person has grown old, he must inevitably turn to self-rejection, self-abasement, and self-hatred. On the other hand, a different orientation, espoused by gerontologists, would promote acquiring a set of attitudes that will enable one to appreciate each stage of life as it comes along.

Because the aged must turn with mounting necessity to the medical profession, negative attitudes toward aging and the aged among medical specialists can cause serious psychological damage. Morris is aware of the feelings of hopelessness, gloom, and futility that can be conveyed to the aged by doctors, psychologists, social workers, and even teachers and ministers.[12]

On the positive side, there is evidence that some medical schools do not regard their students as fully trained until they have been sensitized to both the physical and the sociopsychological changes that occur in the aged. With such knowledge, technicians and specialists will be less apt to regard their services as wasted or unproductive when they are assigned to work with elderly patients.

Learning Ability

The stereotyped image of an older person is that of a rigid, cautious, intellectually weak and uninterested person who will avoid the new and unfamiliar. The evidence continues to mount, however, that this simplistic notion is not supported by empiric investigation. Much depends upon what is meant by "intelligence," "rigidity," and "adaptability." These are not qualities that lend themselves to easy definition and measurement. Most investigators distinguish a variety of components and related factors that affect the total results. Chief among these is speed of performance. This factor is one that is rewarded in American society and tends to favor younger persons.[13]

But when it comes to such matters as vocabulary or information, which can be acquired only with time, older persons have given the superior performances. Trembly and O'Connor, for example, reported the results of mental tests on an impressive number of subjects—33,283 males ranging from age six to past sixty.[14] They found that "scores on English vocabulary, a measure of acquired knowledge, rose rapidly during the early years, then more slowly, but never reached a plateau, nor declined. In contrast, scores on the aptitude tests rose rapidly during the early years, reached a plateau, then declined."[15]

Abilities with hearing tones matured at age ten, held a plateau for about thirty-five years, and then began to decline at about age forty-five. Ability to work with designs matured at fourteen, held fairly stable for about eighteen years, and began to falter at about age thirty-two. Dealing with numbers showed maturity at eighteen, endured for a short nine years, and began to decline at age twenty-seven. Inductive reasoning was the aptitude that matured latest, but it was also earliest to decline, peaking only briefly between the ages of twenty-one and twenty-three.[16] The theory Trembly and O'Connor advance is that "the earliest appearing traits in the individual . . . show longer plateaus and decline at older ages than the later-appearing traits."[17]

Perhaps the real test of the powers of older persons to meet changed conditions should not be based upon contrived mental tests, but rather upon such meaningful tasks as adapting to industrial changes in occupation. An oil refinery, for example, made a change to automation that required retraining its production workers and instrument operators, who were all aged fifty or older. The grades they achieved in the retraining did not differ essentially, and the span was further minimized if level of education was taken into account.[18] By contrast, when long-distance telephone operators had to be retrained to use an IBM card instead of the more familiar paper form, the older employees did not do as well as the younger because rapid changes in psychomotor activity were required and these have generally been found to work against older persons.[19]

Birren has offered a succinct summary of much research concerning the intellectual powers of older persons:

> As progress is made in research on the analysis of logical problem-solving behavior of persons over a wide age range, it will be possible to specify the individual differences in the sequence between some problem input and the resulting solution, or behavioral output. These sequences will no doubt be found to differ with age between the healthy person of high initial ability and with good education and supporting environment and the individual with poor health, low initial ability, poor education, and an unsupporting environment. At present there are only intimations about the nature of these efforts.[20]

The unraveling of the tangled skein of biological changes, psychological attributes, and social factors complicates the problem of fully understanding aging individuals. Which are causes and which are effects may not yet be known, but their mutually reinforcing impacts are apparent. Inaccessibility to health services for rural persons, fewer visits to physicians and dentists by the poor and uninformed, isolation through social distance because of racial discrimination, and urban anonymity number among the social factors that combine to remove many aged from the kind of healthy, active, and purposeful life that gerontologists envision as possible for many older individuals.

Contingencies or Predisposing Factors

MENTAL ILLNESS

One of the great fears that haunt the aged is the loss of mental faculties. A clear mind is the most precious entity, in the declarations of the elderly. Their physical strength may wane, but their ability to speak and act within normal limits is paramount.

Unfortunately, as individuals age, chances increase that mental disorder or inacceptable psychological functioning will occur. Such symptoms of psychological disturbance as deviations from normal behavior or bizarre verbalizations are often tolerated by close associates. That an aging person has crossed the line between usual behavior and intolerable behavior may not be recognized for some time because persons close to him are aware of his idiosyncracies and do not "read" them negatively. However, if his behavior becomes too disturbing, admission to some mental facility for diagnosis and therapy is usually forthcoming. Aging is apparently highly related to mental aberrations, for approximately 40 percent of new admissions into mental institutions are over sixty years of age.

Mental difficulties, of course, cover a vast range, including acute brain disorders resulting from toxic reactions to infections, drugs, or chemicals; tumors, head injuries, circulatory disturbances, or metabolic changes; and chronic brain disorders caused by permanent impairment of cerebral tissue from infection, poisonous agents, trauma, cerebral arteriosclerosis, and senile dementia. Functional disorders may result from menopause, manic-depressive states, paranoia, and psychophysiological disorders. Other common symptoms associated with aging include hypochondriasis (anxious preoccupation with the body), insomnia, wandering, irritability, and hostility.[21]

For the less-serious disorders that lend themselves to therapeutic correction such as drug therapy, psychoanalysis, or shock therapy, there is often sufficient improvement in the patient's behavior to justify release from institutional care. For the aged who experience serious damage to the brain or nervous system and who are deprived of economic resources, the period of institutional care may be prolonged and is frequently more custodial than therapeutic in nature. First admissions of the aged to public mental hospitals alone are projected at approximately 48,000 by 1975—a decided increase in institutionalized aged in the future.[22]

LIFE CHANCES IN SOCIAL CLASSES

Despite protestations to the contrary, social stratification exists in most societies and will dictate the degree of access to goods and services. Each individual has much of his life determined for him by the relative flexibility or rigidity of the class system in which he finds himself. It is important to know the "starting point" in a person's life; for his class—upper, middle, or lower—will set the stage for his lifelong habits, interests, motivations, training, and values. Thereafter, an individual may become upwardly mobile, downwardly oriented, or fairly stable.

In the upper classes, the central mode is to maintain status, to gracefully accept the beneficences of past generations, or to emulate one's past quietly, tastefully, conservatively, and effectively. Middle-class orientation is toward obedience, harmony, and future success. Ownership of a substantial home, comfortable conditions, and some protection from crises are middle-class goals. At the lower socioeconomic levels, the stress is on sheer survival, aggressiveness, and physical vigor.

Escape from reality is understandably a part of lower-class life. Facing reality is regarded as the most courageous posture among the middle class. For the upper classes, reality is chiefly a matter of selecting from a rather wide range of options that can help one savor and enjoy the artistic and beautiful in life. All these characteristics of social strata have meaningful implications in the lives of aging individuals.

One could hypothesize that the circumstances of lower-class life would produce a maximum of mental distress. A major study in New Haven, Connecticut, by Hollingshead and Redlich, confirms such a close association between social class and mental illness.[23] Six state hospitals, five veterans' hospitals, eleven general hospitals with psychiatric wards, and seven clinics made their records available to this sociologist and psychiatrist team. In addition, forty-six private practitioners in the study area cooperated with the research team. The two populations—the patients and a 5 percent sample of New Haven households—were stratified into five class categories. All classes were underrepresented in the patient population except the lower class, which had 38.2 percent of the patients but constituted only 18.4 percent of the nonpatient population. The lower class appeared twice as frequently among the patients. Further, serious psychoses occurred with greater frequency among the lower classes and led to long-term custodial care at public expense for those patients judged to be senile.

Since 1956, the National Health Survey of the National Center for Health Statistics, a unit of the U.S. Public Health Service, has employed national sampling techniques on a continuing basis to determine individual medical records of illness, chronic conditions, injuries, examinations, treatments, preventive care, and their ultimate effects. Some 42,000 interviews are conducted annually. The first examination cycle was completed in 1962 and involved 6,672 representative adults aged eighteen to seventy-nine. The second cycle covered 1962 to 1965 and collected data on a representative sample of 7,000 children aged six to eleven. Currently, examinations are going forward in four mobile trailers with children between twelve and seventeen.[24]

The findings of the National Health Survey clearly confirm that

> there is a positive relation between poor health and low income. . . . For people in families with a total income of less than $2,000 a year

there were (in 1961) 29 days of restricted activity per year per person. For those with a family income in the $2,000 to $4,000 range the number of disability days dropped to 18, and in families with an income of more than $4,000 the number was 13.

. . .

On the basis of information gathered between mid-1963 and mid-1964, 59 percent of the people with family income of less than $2,000 had consulted a physician at least once during the preceding year. The proportion of the population with one visit or more to physicians rose steadily with income. It was 66 percent for people in families with $4,000 to $7,000 a year, 73 percent in families with $10,000 or more.[25]

Finally, the National Health Survey found "the number of dental appointments per capita (perhaps one of the best indexes of elective health care) is more than three times as high for upper-income groups as for lowest-income groups."[26]

Birren probed behind this quantitative data when he wrote:

One of the important implications is that late in life the reactions of individuals to death of spouse, retirement, reduced income, and loss of social role and physical prowess will be in terms of long-developing values, values that have their roots in class differences and in particular family constellations. It might be expected from this that aged lower class individuals would prove to be antagonistic but passive in the face of age changes. Middle class individuals would be more "hurt" by the psychological implications of the changes. To this extent, social class origins and mobility influence the way an individual ages, the way in which he reacts to the characteristic changes of later life and to particular age-related problems; i.e., whether he is highly controlled or aggressively impulsive.

. . . Failure to reach early goals would be a psychological problem for the aspiring middle class man about to retire, but not for the lower class man who would probably blame his employers or others for what he might consider a "bad deal."[27]

At many moments in life, there are critical choices to be made. Should one leave home and seek more stimulating experiences? What educational programs should be followed? What vocations and avocations should one pursue? What friendships should be cultivated, and which persons should be avoided? Whom should one marry?

The alternatives are many, and young people need as much guidance as possible. For upper-class persons, aids are generally available and role uncertainty is minimized. For middle-class persons, however, role potentials are not so easily handled or easily changed if one is overcommitted. For the lower classes, effective guidance to counterbalance the depressing circumstances of poverty is generally lacking. The dilemmas of selecting roles are not confronted, and the usual path is adapting to a threatening and physically demanding life.[28]

Elderly individuals at each class level can recite, and often do, crucial moments of decision when the conscious or unconscious selection of a course of action set the tone for the remainder of their lives. They can lucidly recall over many years the choice that was "the best thing I ever did" or "the most foolish move I ever made." Long-range euthenic efforts to provide "ladders by which to climb" for as many people as possible could undoubtedly alter drastically the current gloom and despondency that troubles so many older Americans. For older Americans of the future, such situations of lifelong regret and recriminations need not occur.

Facing Life

As the years flow by and aging individuals continue to move in the directions that their circumstances have set for them, they become aware of the situations over which they can exercise some control and of those that are beyond their power. A brief look at a few selected factors that can lengthen or shorten life will help illustrate how individuals can determine the quantity and quality of their years.

OBESITY

For many persons, one of the obvious changes in later years is a gain in weight. This poses no serious danger to life until such time as there is excessive fat deposition and its ensuing physical and psychological strain. Obesity seems to plague older women, although women seem to be more conscientious than men about weight control. Interestingly, women generally have a greater amount of adipose tissue than men, and yet their survival rate exceeds that of men. If excess fat is deleterious to health and longevity, it would appear that this additional weight would work against females. Apparently, adipose tissue has some survival value, and other factors, such as what constitutes "excess weight" or hormonal balances, are at work.

The heavy-set man may traditionally be regarded as "jolly," but the shortening of life because of excess tissue is a most serious matter. Weight increases are usually tied to overeating, a simplistic but true deduction. But what motivates a person to consume much more than he needs? It is known that when psychological insight is applied, the craving for a heavy intake of food can be reduced considerably. The causes of obesity have been attributed to such things as metabolic changes, sedentary living, reaction to tensions, substitute gratifications, food addiction, and neurotic defenses. When these are understood and handled properly, obesity can be controlled.[29]

SMOKING

The general public was alerted to the dangers of tobacco smoking, particularly cigarette smoking, by a 1964 report of the Advisory Committee of the Public Health Service to the Surgeon General.[30] Tobacco smoking was identified as being *causally* related to cancer of the lung, larynx, and lip and to chronic bronchitis. Other diseases *associated* with smoking, but not regarded as causally related, are arteriosclerotic heart disease (including coronary disease), cirrhosis of the liver, emphysema, stomach ulcers, cancer of the esophagus, cancer of parts of the oral cavity other than the lip, cancer of the bladder and other urinary organs, and certain noncoronary cardiovascular diseases.[31]

Women did not begin to smoke cigarettes in significant numbers until about the 1920s and 1930s, and only a third of their numbers did so. Men have shown a pattern of smoking at an early age, and about two-thirds of their numbers smoke. For a time, death rates associated with smoking correlated closely with these factors, but recently women have begun to exceed men in incidence of lung cancer. Any natural or inherent advantages women may possess in longevity are wiped out by adoption of the cigarette habit.

The "devil may care" attitude of many persons who have been confronted with these data has been that the "price" of smoking is worth the satisfaction derived. They may cite air pollution or automobile accidents as other life-shortening factors as well and point out that few will leave crowded cities to escape their effects. There are apparently certain areas over which people have little inclination to exercise alternative action, regardless of how harmful their present course may be. In the case of smoking, however, there does seem to be some margin of personal choice.

MARITAL STATUS

Another factor of longevity is marital status; a married person can expect about an additional five years of life. Many wits have remarked that this longevity is not really so, "it only seems that much longer." But the longer survival of married couples need not be treated facetiously; the facts are there, abetted by a number of related factors. In the first place, those in good health are more likely to be chosen for matrimony. Further, the improved nutrition from well-chosen foods prepared with care on a regular basis, comfortable housing or at least efforts to make it so, the exercise of caution because of added responsibilities, prompt attention to warning signals of ill health, and social approval for the release of tensions through a considerate partner contribute to increased survival. However, if such factors are not found in a marriage, then marital status does little to prolong survival.

SUICIDE

One way for a frustrated person to eliminate his frustration is to remove himself from his distressing situation by self-destruction. More appropriate procedure in terms of facing life might be to resolve the painful problem, if possible, to attain a minimum of self-satisfaction and ease. Although suicides occur at different ages, a striking feature of suicide statistics is the sex-differential pattern for aging men and women. A ten-year summary of suicides in the United States from 1954 through 1963 demonstrated that the suicide rate was highest for men sixty-five years old and over and for women between the ages of forty-five and sixty-four.[32] This corresponds with the "role-less" roles of men in retirement and of women in menopausal change of life—people who are lonely, depressed, perhaps seriously ill, and unable to cope with the stresses that age brings. They contemplate only a bleak, empty future. Aging per se is not causative of suicide, but it is contributive in the sense that it is the end product in a lifelong series of circumstances that can set the stage for the final tragic episode of self-obliteration.

Facing Death

Certainly one of the most difficult personal problems in living is to come to grips with the inevitability of one's own demise. In this mental exercise, individuals develop various ways of turning away from their involvement in life. Each settles upon some pattern that will enable him to be functional despite the certainty of eventual loss of his conscious "self." Perhaps no other pattern reflects more of the personality organization than the manner in which a person approaches his own death.

Religion may offer some comfort to those who view death as the entrance into eternal "life." Many may pay lip service to religious views, but the mystery of death continues to be a gnawing puzzle. Some turn away from contemplating their own death because they consider death-denial preferable to morbid and depressing preoccupation with matters beyond their control. An interesting pattern is to taunt death, as Spanish matadors or Halloween revelers do. In this form of bravado, the horrible and the macabre are converted into demonstrations of joyous fearlessness, which wins the approval of the timid and the fearful. Or, for those who have endured much, death is welcomed as a release from toil and strife. This pattern is expressed more by the elderly than by the young.

For the young, selfhood is emerging, and they are somewhat intoxicated with its power. For the aged, however, nothing remains but the mounting evidence of the fragility and minuteness of selfhood. The inability of the self to comprehend its own end slowly dawns upon one's consciousness, because where death exists, the self has vanished. For whatever comfort may be derived, an individual can surmise what his works may mean to those who will possess life after him.

Supporting the notion that the young must take precedence over the old is the potential future that lies before them. There is a futurity to youth that can lift their spirits beyond present reversals. If life has dealt them trying times, there are many years left to alter their course and achieve a better life. At the root of the unconcern for the aged lies their highly limited future. What return is assured society for whatever is done to make their lives more comfortable or pleasant? In a weakened, vegetative state, the aged do not promise much to an investing society. Demands for euthanasia are occasionally heard, but they are usually stifled by man's deep commitment to life, no matter how difficult, painful, or limited. In the valiant efforts to sustain life, there is a clear recognition that the miracle of life ranks as one of man's highest values and cannot be destroyed with impunity.

Summation

Social gerontology as an emerging specialty is concerned, in part, with how the aging process affects individuals, not so much in a subjective sense but in an objective sense. This is no simple task in the face of the wide diversity of aging persons.

Basic to all aging individuals are physical changes, internal and external, that slowly but inevitably diminish personal powers so laboriously secured over the years. Neither the same effects nor the same rates of decline apply equally to all aging persons. Whatever changes are manifested, attitudes toward self and toward others are of paramount concern. Chief among the possible attitude sets is a youth-centeredness that undervalues and stigmatizes the elderly. This perspective not only pervades a self-view of aging but also reduces the effectiveness of professional counseling services.

The physical "stigmata" of growing old are allegedly accompanied by losses in learning ability, but this perspective ignores the considerable intellectual strength found among older persons. Aging alone does not account for the range of talents among the aged; biological changes, psychological attributes, and contributive societal factors interplay to explain ultimate outcome.

Contingencies that predispose individuals to various ends include encounters with mental illness and placement in a socioeconomic level that may or may not permit mobility or escape from restrictive circumstances. The close correlation between social class and health is suggestive of multiple causes operative for life histories.

Aging individuals confront both life and death because they are near the end of one and the beginning of the other. Obesity, smoking, marital status, and suicide are among the factors that alter a life span. Subtle psychological mechanisms determine how one contemplates death. These mirror personality organization and take on mounting importance as death nears.

Perhaps the real difference between young and old is the unlimited future that stretches ahead for the young and the brief time left for the aged. Even when life seems empty and painful to the elderly, it is usually valiantly preserved.

CHAPTER *SEVEN*

Aging and Society

Around the nuclei of universal confrontations, every society has evolved specific patterns that reflect its ethos or system of values. Aging and its products are one of these universal conditions with which each society must come to terms. From the broader perspective of examining a macrosystem, Wilbert Moore sees three "pervasive conditions," subject, of course, "to the effects of human ingenuity and the unplanned consequences of human action."[1] These are "*numbers:* the demographic dimensions of societies; *space:* the ecological concentration and dispersion of human populations; and *time:* the temporal boundaries of life and the sequential ordering of action."[2] These pervasive conditions have considerable relevance for social gerontology in terms of both research and theory.

In societies characterized by brief life spans and precarious survival, aging as a significant process tends to receive minimal social attention. At best, the few who outlive their contemporaries are generally objects of awe and esteem. But in those societies that have marshaled their forces sufficiently to preserve even frail individuals under fairly optimal conditions, aging has emerged as a problem that can no longer be treated as a side issue. The latter half of the twentieth century, at least, has been notable among Western societies in the conscious and concerted efforts calculated to cope with the aged and their increasing millions.

A Latent Function of Society

It is rather doubtful that societies deliberately set the goal of the survival of millions of aging persons as one of their prime objectives. Rather, conscious consideration of social gerontological phenomena was most likely a by-product clamoring for attention in societies whose telic objectives were rarely in clear sight. Aging, in this sense, is more a latent function than it is a manifest function of societies.

An opposing view, however, would hold that growing concern with aging did not "just happen." Instead, many legitimately argue that aging as a phenomenon never really passed unnoticed and undesired among men and that it received appropriate attention as its impact became obvious. Perhaps one of the central distinctions between mankind and other animals is that men are keenly aware of time and have taken its toll into account in their social structures.

An interesting study by Michael Wallach and Leonard Green underscores the increasing value placed upon time by older subjects in contrast with younger subjects matched for education and intelligence.[3] To the older subjects, time was associated with "swift metaphors" such as "a speeding train," "a fleeing thief," or "a galloping horseman," while younger subjects associated time with "a vast expanse of sky," "the Rock of Gibraltar," or "a quiet, motionless ocean."

During an early symposium focusing on the social contributions by the aging, the effective use of whatever time remained for older persons was discussed. Judged subjectively as fleeting by the aging, but objectively as prolonged by younger members of society, time was treated as unthreatening to neither the aging nor their society if supportive measures were taken. The consensus among the contributors was that

> most older people can and will maintain themselves as self-sufficient members of society once they are given the opportunity. Thus, edu-

cation, housing, community services, health promotion and rehabilitation, income maintenance, activity programs, and employment counseling are seen as just normal community facilities, as are elementary, secondary, and college education, pediatric clinics, vocational counseling, playgrounds, and clubs for children and young adults. They are not to be regarded as welfare services in the sense of ministering to psychologically, medically, and financially dependent old people, but rather seen as part of the environment through which we make normal adjustments to the changes and circumstances of the later years.[4]

This philosophy of aging continues to be a binding thread running through much of social gerontology. Aging persons are seen as active participants in the total societal milieu provided a society does not give priority to "more pressing business" and invest its resources elsewhere. War, for example, may be so demanding that persons of all ages may be expendable, and attention to sheer preservation of the social order takes precedence over concern for any one segment.

Not only has aging required some type of response from societies, but it has, in turn, been profoundly affected by the reaction each society has had to its presence. The relations between the aged and their society are, thus, mutually reinforcing or reciprocal. As the elderly become a fixed segment of society, societal organization takes their presence into account. In turn, depending upon what limitations are imposed, the aged form self-images.

Models of Age Grading and Their Strains

Theoretically, there are at least seven different combinations of age grading or age distinctions that a society might select as appropriate models. These permutations involve "the old generation," socially defined as "retired persons" in the United States but not necessarily elsewhere; "the middle generation," or the "economically active"; and "the young," usually preadolescent and economically active only in a peripheral sense. There is nothing sacrosanct about these divisions; they are arbitrary distinctions and may be separated by periods of many years in some cases. They are used only as heuristic constructs to simplify analysis of variant forms of including or excluding the aging in a society. They are:

1. Domination by the elderly, or a geritocracy
2. Domination by the middle-aged
3. Domination by the young
4. Submergence or subordination of the young by the middle generation and the elderly, age being an asset
5. Glorification of nonproductivity, in which the young and the old may enjoy a life supported by the middle generation
6. Isolation of the elderly in favor of the young and the middle generation
7. Cooperation, coupled with appreciation, among all age grades

The first type, domination by the aged, has enjoyed historical acceptance in Europe and much of Asia. It is the pattern that some aged in America nostalgically expected would be their lot. Homage and the power they hoped to wield would automatically follow as they reached seniority. Such persons had been content in subordination and service to the older persons who provided for their needs as children and adolescents.

Immigrants to America have been appalled to observe the separation or widening gulf between generations to the point of alienation, bitterness, and abandonment. Other immigrants, however, anticipated normative changes in growing old and knowingly prepared for their "twilight years." An "independent" old age, in the sense of not relying upon the largesse of other generations, is the sworn objective of certain aging persons who believe they have realistically assessed their situation.

There is strain in this geriocentric model, as perhaps there is in any so-called equilibrium. These strains seethe beneath the surface of stabilized societies and occasionally boil to the surface if conditions permit. John Thompson, a photographer in China in 1860, encountered such a condition. He was aware that the Chinese believed that cameras could cause death—an "evil eye" concept not unknown in other societies. He was not surprised to find "portraits of children difficult to obtain."[5] But he thought it strange that "in a land where filial piety is esteemed the highest of virtues, sons and daughters brought their aged parents to be placed before the foreigner's silent and mysterious instrument of destruction."

The second model, domination by the middle-aged, refers to the critical and decision-laden status of "the middle generation," which neither is preparing to enter adult responsibilities nor has retired from them. Despite the youth orientation of American society, the middle generations both determine and carry out plans in behalf of all age grades.

The enormous teen-age market is commonly cited as evidence of domination by the adolescent in America. This market grows and prospers, however, chiefly because mature persons are willing to cater to adolescent whims. A study by Kathryn Powell and David Gover notes that over $9 billion is spent annually by teen-age consumers.[6] Powell and Gover's investigation of 12,317 white males and females from the seventh, ninth, and twelfth grades from a stratified sample of urban and rural public schools in South Carolina indicated that over half received their money from parents with no work required of them. In addition, these youngsters had complete freedom to spend their money as they pleased. Those with charge accounts in their own name ran as high as 40 percent for twelfth-grade boys and 20 percent for girls.[7]

It is true that these young people began to learn money management by such tactics, but the power of assent to these arrangements was still vested in the parental middle generation. It should be noted, in addition, that when conditions make it desirable to control teen-agers, there is little hesitancy among the middle-aged to exercise discretionary powers. In such matters as adolescent conformity to school or college requirements, enforcement of community laws, and conscription for military service, youngsters are not necessarily consulted. On the one hand, children and adolescents find middle-aged persons willing to be generous. On the other hand, they may cry out in dismay when they discover their demands are not viewed as "profitable" to the middle-aged and, hence, left unsatisfied. The strain in this model may be observed in such tactics as draft-card burnings, sit-ins, speak-outs, teach-ins, and flights to foreign countries. Protests may be encouraged and tolerated for a time, but, in the end, the middle generation will determine which course of action to pursue.

The third model, domination by the young, represents rather complete default of both the middle and older generations. The assumption of social power, however, is more subtle than direct "takeover." This "the child is king" philosophy employs the idea of the strength of a chain lying ultimately in its weakest link. On a small scale, this model is seen in a family of adults centering their activities on the needs of a newly arrived and "helpless" infant. Family schedules are altered for the sake of the child. On a larger scale, child-centeredness becomes child orientation and child domination. Because "the formative years" of youth are known to be so vital to later life, older generations make concessions tantamount to surrender of prerogatives. "Young Turks" have been instrumental in shifting the seat of power in a society, but their periods of power are relatively short. Revolutionaries also age and resent challenges to the social order they established when young.

In the fourth model, in which the middle generation and the elderly join forces to subdue the young, age is an asset; there is greater continuity than is possible under a geritocracy. The strains in this model are associated with satisfying two generations, but subordinating the third "supplying," or "reserve," generation.

The fifth model, which turns from productivity or work and glorifies nonproductivity, is advocated by many as the most reasonable and satisfying. It returns the elderly to the "playing" status of the young. The young and the old may enjoy life while the "working" middle generation supports them. Grandparents and grandchildren may be joined in common cause while working parents provide all the essentials as well as the luxuries. The middle generation may be invited to join in the fun of occasional vacations or weekends, provided they finance activities. The middle generation may find consolation if they can be convinced of the joys of their labors, but they may envy the young and the old whose time schedules are more flexible than their own.

The sixth model, isolation of the elderly, would be rejected by many older persons. It casts them out of society, subtly or not so subtly, leaving them to find refuge elsewhere. Such isolation or disengagement is not acceptable to those acclimated to productive activity. It should be clear, of course, that the elderly are not unanimous in their resentment toward other generations for removing them from useful work. Many elderly welcome release from the social harnesses that tied them to impersonal productivity. A gerontologist from Puerto Rico has observed that retirement is freely translated as jubilation for those workers who prefer their ease to the tedium of their former labors in factories and fields. It has already been noted that in preliterate societies, elders have delightfully and artfully deceived younger generations by convincing food gatherers that the elders' consumption of certain foods works ultimately for the good of the more vigorous.[8]

The final model, cooperation among all age groups, is an idealistic one in which all age grades have equal status, appreciate each other, and work for the good of all. This utopian concept may or may not be possible, but it holds the promise of emphasizing the contributions of each generation and neglecting none. It is a far cry from the individual-centeredness promoted in the United States and would be resented by those who fear group dominations for the sake of social order.

None of these "models" exists in a pure state in any society; rather, they flow together at times and represent the different alternatives that societies follow as circumstances change. All seem to have distinctive strains because heterogeneity exists in greater measure than homogeneity.

Conflict and Cooperation Between Generations

Aging is constantly bringing new generations into being and, with each generation, a unique set of experiences. In American society, "the Roaring Twenties," "the Depression Thirties," "the Warring Forties," "the Postwar Fifties," and "the Soaring Sixties" serve as examples. In each of these decades, the rearing of children differed. Previously, generations were separated by a thirty-year interval, the span between childhood dependency and adult independence. But in urban societies marked by rapid upheavals, the thousands born and raised amid significant changes are different enough to be marked off from each other by intervals of approximately ten years.

In preliterate societies, characterized by minimum social change, children are grouped in age grades, two or three years apart, which experience joint initiations into adult status. The closest modern equivalent to these age grades would be children who enter school grades year by year, class by class, separated from each other by less than twelve months. Friendships might occur between classes, but the most intense relationships develop within the classes that eventually graduate together.

With varying periods of time from thirty years to less than one year separating generations, the potential for conflict, cooperation, or some form of "antagonistic cooperation" between generations is present. Rebellious youth may chafe under the authority of older generations whom they judge too "imprinted" with the past and less "impressed" with the present. This would reach exaggerated form under conditions of rapid change. Folk societies, at the other extreme, characterized by resistance to change and orientation toward time-tested and venerable patterns, would have younger generations well in hand and convinced that the older generations were truly repositories of wisdom and worthy of respect and emulation.

Only contact with contrasting culture patterns could provide seeds of suspicion that the old, familiar ways may not be the best. In this context, the injunction "Be ye not yoked with unbelievers" makes good sense. Pauline Young's brilliant study of the Molokans illustrates how this principle works to maintain group continuity. Ingroup solidarity was diminished in proportion to the generous treatment accorded younger Molokans in Los Angeles, the reverse of the cruelties suffered by their parents and grandparents in their search for cultural integrity.[9] A recent study by Bernard Rosen of Jewish teen-agers in American society makes the identical point.[10] In the more tolerant and permissive atmosphere of America, Jewish separatism demands even greater loyalty than when anti-Semites are intent upon Judaic oblivion.

Competing generations may regard the surrender of power between generations as not rapid enough. In consciously age-graded societies, the acquisition of power is assured through various rites of passage into stratified organizations. Among the Mandan of North Dakota, for example, age-graded organizations leading up to the top-ranking Buffalo Bulls existed, but prestige and power were both earned and purchased through members of higher-ranked associations.[11] The Apinayé of eastern Brazil have four distinctive age sets: "boys who have not been initiated into adult status; warriors between the ages of fifteen and twenty-five years; mature men who have passed through warrior status; and elders who are no longer active in log racing [an endurance contest in which huge logs are carried for as much as ten miles]."[12]

The Nyakyusa of the Great Rift Valley of Africa at the north end of Lake Nyasa are a distinctive society in terms of their recognition of rivalry between age grades. The Nyakyusa develop outlying villages of herders about ten or eleven years of age separate from the parents' villages. Other boys of similar age from neighboring villages join them for about five years, after which the village is closed to newcomers. The age span between the men in these villages is thus about five years. Each village, usually numbering between twenty and fifty members, lasts a lifetime and consists of the small group of founding boys, their wives, and their dependents. Once during each generation, a major ritual formally provides for the transfer of power to the younger generation. Land is reallocated, and the elders move away even if the land is not wanted by the younger generation.[13]

Such patterns avoid conflict and ensure a smooth transfer of power between generations. "Retirement" generally begins at age thirty-five for the Nyakyusa, a far cry from the clinging to positions well past the age of sixty-five in Western societies. Both the blurring of the demarcation lines between generations and the unstructured situation that produces the anxiety, uncertainty, and resentment can be credited for the not-so-smooth transfer of power between generations in urban societies. Even if there is consensus that older generations must relinquish power, just which forms should be followed puzzles many would-be reformers.

The Aged—Subculture or Contraculture?

Whether eased out, forced out, or moved out by mutual agreement, older generations are confronted with a vast amount of uncommitted time, especially in the United States. What may be developing among older persons is a "consciousness of kind" resulting from their common experience as a quasi minority. Perhaps the separate-but-equal doctrine will be invoked next, a dead-end alternative acceptable to the young but not necessarily to the old. A value shift toward leisure activity, however, appears to hold promise for the aged. In this, the young, the middle-aged, and the old are more likely to agree. Some have called the aged the most fortunate generation because they are truly "pioneers in leisure."[14]

Some concerned with the economy, however, fear the elderly as a contraculture that can drain business and industry by incessant demands for support during their nonproductive years. Unlike funded private pension plans or insurance, the social security system is based on "assessmentism," the assessing of current workers to pay for the support or persons who did not or could not provide for their later years. This particular criticism does not concern itself with profit taking when the elderly are financially solvent, nor does it deal with what part the elderly played in reaching current levels of economic strength. The unfavorable economic position of many elderly may not be due to shortsightedness, willfulness, or lack of initiative but to circumstances altogether disassociated from aging.[15] Creeping inflation will diminish the buying power of a fixed income, for example. Certainly, inflation is no great asset to those of younger generations who are still economically active. Strategy must deal more with social conditions in general than with those persons who are less than fortunate under the status quo.

Time and Social Systems

The passage of time works not only upon individuals but also upon those systems that individuals create in order to live. Families, voluntary associations, business and industrial networks, educational ties, professional liaisons, and social movements number among the person-to-person relationships that progress in complexity ultimately to institutional systems and total societies. The survival of these entities of sociological concern is not dependent upon individuals who come and go. In this sense, social relationships or systems have a "life" of their own; man has apparently produced "immortal" congeries.

However, "death-free" systems may be in various states of social health. Thus, there are those social systems that provide for the smooth replacement of individual participants, for their recruitment, training, and services as well as for their withdrawal. Such "life-sustaining" entities would be universities, corporations, agencies, armies, and religious organizations. These activities may be compared with the sustained cellular repair and replacement of living organs. Social movements, for example, that flourish only through the leadership of some charismatic personality are bound to fail with his demise. Those that provide for more prosaic organizational leaders, however, form an unbreakable chain of committed persons that transcends many lifetimes.[16]

Adaptability is also characteristic of surviving systems. In biological evolution, those creatures that became overspecialized or overly adapted in their behavior range are now fossils. Homo sapiens is the current beneficiary of the evolutionary process because his adaptations were never so extreme that he could not move on with changed conditions.[17] In the publishing field, a book requires continuous revision to survive profitably, or it will suffer the fatal "disease" of being dated. Applied to social systems, provisions for survival include amendment, revision, and reorientation. To do otherwise is to guarantee obsolescence.

Finally, transfer of information between integral parts of a system also affects its survival. Biologists are familiar with the failure of the "messenger" RNA particles to carry the biochemical codes from the DNA double helix to the rest of the body cells. The results are mutants, which may or may not be capable of survival. The "communication gap" between generations is an example of this same principle. Unfamiliarity with the triumphs and failures of past generations forces existing generations to begin all over again, marking time until some forward motion can be found.

Wilbert Moore offers four typological cases dealing with this "communication gap" that associate aging individuals with changing social systems and so provide instructive gerontological conceptualizations.[18]

The first type consists of those traditional societies in which change is relatively slow and each succeeding generation experiences similar time-tested conditions. In this type, models for role behavior are available and may be merely imitated. Both aging individuals and their associated social systems may be said to be "adjusted" at various levels of efficiency.

The second type involves more rapid social change, requiring older individuals to hurry a bit to keep up with changed circumstances. This requires "refresher" courses and "retooling" because others have made major innovations. A familiar case is those women who have interrupted their education to have families and who return to school to catch up on developments during their absence. The same applies to professionals whose formal training is over but who must keep up with their expanding fields as best they can. This puts pressure on aging individuals who do keep pace, but with attendant costs.

Moore's third type is the accelerated social change that forces aging individuals to drop out of the competitive struggle. In this case, the young innovators are indeed dominant and the aged are rejected personalities who do not "fit" new conditions.

The fourth type is social change so rapid that it not only makes the elderly obsolete but also displaces the young. In this type, the "aging" is not reserved for those sixty years of age or older but weighs heavily upon those thirty and forty years of age, which, according to Moore, is the case in contemporary industrialized societies. The young and the old now find themselves allied in a common cause to keep pace with systems that have raced ahead of them.

Inclusion or Exclusion in Society

The ghost that haunts older persons and their allies is the development of social policy that may lead to their exclusion from the social order. In primitive societies, there appears to be no "aging problem." In industrial societies, however, events in time produce changes that seriously threaten aging individuals.

One answer, reminiscent of the age-graded villages of the Nyakyusa, is the voluntary ecological pattern of living in age-similar communities. However, if residence in such places is involuntary, their worth is diminished because freedom and individual dignity have been violated.

For many years, rural America, while never enthusiastic, was resigned to keeping the old folks "down on the farm" or taking the indigent elderly "over the hill to the poor farm." But rural living for the elderly is neither as idyllic nor as easy as some would believe. Even those with a lifetime of rural living behind them have found country or farm community living increasingly distressing.[19] Rural nonfarm communities have gained in popularity, but, even with increased amenities, living in these places has also proved vexing to many older persons.

The variety of choices open to American elderly in determining where to live in retirement mirrors the diversity of their ranks. Trailers, modest homes, high-rise apartments, hotels, and retirement communities may be found in practically every state and operate under a variety of auspices from private to public and from religious to secular, in rural and urban areas, in narrow to wide age ranges, and with widely varying health, educational, and recreational facilities.[20]

Major moves normally are made after much deliberation and weighing of alternatives. Older persons may willingly prepare for such a move but will be filled with doubts if the pressure to change residence comes from profit-motivated persons.[21] With a buying power of some $40 billion, older Americans have often been the dupes of unscrupulous sellers.[22] The ensuing anguish among the elderly is not as easily measured as their irretrievable loss in financial power.

Development of Gerontological Specialists

The increasing involvement of personnel to provide the necessary gerontological knowledge and services is a manifestation of just how much society has consciously stirred itself to meet the multiple needs of the aged. Because aging persons are increasing in number and proportion, industrialized Western societies have found persons qualified to deal with the aged in short supply.[23]

One approach has been to enter gerontology through the doors of an established discipline, basic or applied, such as psychology, sociology, economics, political science, medicine, or social work.

Family rehabilitation, counseling, housing, and business administration are also convenient gateways to gerontology. Course offerings leave much to be desired. A student's earliest acquaintance with the formal study of aging usually occurs in passing, more as a footnote to the topic at hand. In brief, the educational goals rarely include gerontological concerns. Interest is kindled only after much academic commitment at the highest level.

Graduate centers in gerontology are being organized to supply the necessary numbers. Prominent among them are the University of Chicago's Training Program in Adult Development and Aging, the University of Michigan's Division of Gerontology, Duke University's Center for Research on Aging, the University of California's Institute of Human Development, the University of Southern California's Institute for Study of Retirement and Aging, and the State University of Iowa's Institute of Gerontology. The Gerontological Society and the American Geriatric Society are among the leading organizations bringing together scholars to consolidate present gerontological knowledge. Gerontology has thus emerged as a society-wide concern shared both by persons high in their profession and by trainees, with the common goal of reaching and understanding the aged.

Operating as liaison are coordinating agencies and organizations that link the aroused public with personnel capable of handling gerontological data. Local, state, and federal levels are represented in community councils, state commissions, and the Administration on Aging.[24] Private organizations such as the National Council on the Aging and the American Association of Retired Persons also provide ample platforms upon which professionals and laymen may meet. Figuratively, the study of aging is in its infancy but from the perspective of its impact on society, there is social ferment of great magnitude.

Summation

Numbers, space, and time are pervasive conditions that limit human societies and are central in understanding social gerontology. Viewed subjectively as brief, but perceived objectively as ever present, time works upon both individuals and the systems in which they live.

There are a minimum of seven different models of age grading from which societies may choose. They consist of domination by the old, the middle-aged, or the young or by some permutation of the three. All contain their satisfactions and their strains. Conflict or cooperation between generations is dependent upon the nature and rate of social changes. If acceptable structures exist to permit the smooth transfer of power between age grades, strains are minimized. Urbanized Western societies are viewed as particularly lacking in smooth transitions and are still in process of evolving them.

The aged have been viewed as a developing contraculture somewhat at odds with their society. What seems more likely is that the aged form a subculture that has not quite adapted to rapid social changes. Practical programs backed by competent personnel are in the making to remedy the situation. In the interim, the aged patiently await their inclusion into or dismissal from society.

CHAPTER *EIGHT*

Social Institutions and Aging

The universal needs of each society include understanding the nature of the circumstances in which it lives; support in terms of food, shelter, and clothing; governing its affairs so that internal harmony can exist and external enemies are repelled; replacement of losses brought about by death, disease, and accidents; rearing of the young to maturity; and amicable relations between the sexes. The systems that attempt to meet these needs are the isomorphisms known as the basic social institutions, such as religion, economy, polity, family, and education. These five are basic enough to constitute an inventory of the orderly forms and procedures found in every society.

Students of social institutions debate their universality, their particular content, and what is acceptable as their exclusive or shared functions. Further, because the conceptualization of social institutions is so broad, or all-encompassing, many other systems or subsystems must be considered. Kinship networks, recreational patterns, artistic expressions, and linguistic exchanges may also be treated as "fundamental." Finally, the range of societal organizations from folk to urban, from family-centered economy to industrialization, and from tribal villages to megalopolises seems to confuse observers further as to the presence or absence of such constructs.

Whereas these issues are the legitimate concern of institutional specialists, students of social gerontology are more concerned with the extent to which each of these broader institutions has effectively dealt with aging and the aged. Have religious organizations, for instance, taken aging and the aged into account or have they treated them as unwelcome burdens added to already heavy responsibilities? Have schools and universities ignored older persons as unworthy, incapable, and decidedly unpromising "consumers" of their educational wares? Have embarrassed or harassed families pushed elder kinsmen aside to get on with the more essential business of rearing children and enjoying adult status after years of dependency? A brief examination of each of these major institutions from the perspective of gerontological studies provides the grist for the mill in this chapter.

Religion and Aging

Perhaps the first time men witnessed death among their kind, saw storms, mighty floods, or volcanic action or recognized their dependence upon game—in short, when men became aware of conditions beyond their control or comprehension—religion was born. Bound together by common agreement that unseen forces were at work upon their lives, men have found solace through faith. Empiric probes may provide increasing clarity and even control over formerly mysterious or frightening prospects, but the increasing knowledge does not nullify established faiths. Instead, it confirms and enriches the conviction that the universe is orderly and unified in the highest spiritual sense. Birth, growth, life, and death tie the aging process intimately to religion in the lives of men.

One might surmise that aging would provoke ambivalent reactions toward organized religion. Much depends, of course, upon how one defines religion or "religiosity." If it is defined as what one does in terms of overt acts of propitiation such as attending services, fulfilling formal duties of piety, or satisfying ritual requirements, then most studies concur that lifetime patterns are not easily broken.[1] Religious youth generally become the religious aged. The nonreligious person, the rebel, the skeptic, and the agnostic also cling tenaciously to habitual patterns as they grow old. Exceptions, of course, only confirm the general rule.

However, if religiosity is defined in terms of covert behavior, such as expression of attitudes toward religion, aging seems to make for significant differences between young and old. Older persons have been found to voice growing disenchantment with formerly satisfying religious concepts. Representative of these studies is a recent one by Edward Ludwig and Robert Eichhorn.[2] Taking dominant American values such as youth orientation to science technology, optimism, and work, Ludwig and Eichhorn reported that faith in the first two values was markedly shaken in their sample of aging Indiana farmers. Faith in a benevolent God or even in the God-given power of man to handle his own affairs adequately was shaken by repeated and cumulative episodes of ill health, pain, and incapacity. For the young, general good health or speedy recovery from difficulties provided ample grounds for belief in the protective and healing powers of the Deity. Unlike patient Job, who was sorely tested and not found wanting, many older persons question the efficacy of pious hopes and cling tenaciously to tangible sources of support, namely, their own hard work.

Supposedly, all ages are welcome in churches and synagogues, but conscious effort is required if the aged are to continue as an integral part of religious activities. Compensating for losses due to aging are such provisions as transportation service, tape recordings of services, radio and television programs for shut-ins, large-print prayer books and hymnals, sound amplifiers, and friendly visiting programs. Public recognition may come in the form of pulpit pronouncements or honorific titles, but, sooner or later, older clergy and laity are required to disengage "gracefully" from active participation.

Overall religious adjustment to the distinctive needs of the aged include appointment of a staff to promote their welfare; publication of papers, magazines, studies, and sermons with gerontological content; sponsorship of seminars and clinics to alert coreligionists to the aging members of their faith; and the administration of hospitals, rest homes, and activity centers in which the aged find positive evidence of religious concern. Although they may be sponsored by a specific religious organization, most facilities for the aged are operated for the good of the entire community and older persons of all religions are welcomed. In this sense, religiously oriented persons see aging as "the great leveler."[3]

There is general agreement in gerontological literature that Jews have provided outstanding leadership in gerontology and geriatrics. Their veneration of aged parents and preservation of filial loyalty are part and parcel of their close family ties. In addition, Judaism itself consciously promotes respect for aging and the aged. This involvement does not imply, however, that Christian concern for the aged is lacking or is remiss. Indeed, both Roman Catholicism and Protestantism have been in the forefront of gerontological promotion. Their contributions have been monumental in terms of institutional care of the aged and educational efforts to anticipate the needs of the aged.[4]

Economics of Aging

Because income is adversely affected by aging, much attention is focused on retirement plans during one's work life. Savings, investments, and pensions constitute the chief sources of income during retirement years and represent the degree of foresight and opportunity operative for individuals and organizations. Savings are defined as sources of ready cash. Investments offer fluctuating returns based on the state of the economy. Pensions provide periodic income for the retired, disabled, dependent, and unemployed. Class differences are perpetuated among the aged because the amount and nature of savings, investments, and pensions correlate with former socioeconomic level. As a general rule, however, income among the aged is reduced from former levels.

Attempts to make up the difference between income during younger years and that received in old age have met with the objection that "a something for nothing" philosophy does not square with overwhelming consensus that income should be in direct proportion to productivity or "worth." If individuals have failed to provide for their retirement years, the responsibility does not fall upon others but continues to rest with the individual. At least so runs the argument. It is true that many cases may be cited of failures to evaluate fully the economic erosions of old age. However, wealth may be "frozen" in property assets, and these may become liabilities because of deteriorating neighborhoods, higher taxation, or costly maintenance.

The indigent remain indigent whether young or old and do wait upon others to redistribute whatever surplus wealth exists. Programs such as Medicare that require contributions before benefits may be realized eliminate the indigent at the outset. As older persons have remarked, "A monthly three-dollar charge is fine for those who have the three dollars." Or, "A hundred-dollar debt on a large hospital bill is certainly a modest requirement, but what do you do if you do not have one hundred cents to your name?" Obviously, other sources of revenue must be tapped and these become, in ascending order, next-of-kin, social-work agencies, counties, states, and the federal government. The nub of the argument turns upon whether economic support for the aged is an "earned" right or an "inherent" right in a democracy. The social security program of the United States, for example, was not conceived as a source of full economic support during old age but was designed to "assist" in income maintenance upon removal from the labor force. Since 1935, however, social security income has become the greatest single source of revenue for the aged and promises to loom into greater importance as "guaranteed and adequate" income levels are established.

Mollie Orshansky has provided an instructive study illustrating the extenuating circumstances under which many poor aged live, particularly when ascriptions are based on persistent and detrimental social definitions.[5] Orshansky places the number of nonwhite aged (sixty-five years and older) in the United States at the end of 1962 at about 1.5 million, or 8 percent of the total aged population. Some 90 percent of these were Negro. She continues:

> Because of their shorter life expectancy and a considerably higher marriage disruption rate, fewer Negroes aged 65 and over than white persons of that age are still married and living with a spouse . . . Considerably more of the Negro women have no husband's income to count on in old age, just as many more of them than white women—according to other data—have earlier lacked a husband's income while raising their children. Because of their inferior earning capacity, more Negro men than white men never marry and so face retirement and old age alone, with no possibility of turning to a wife or grown children to ease health care or financial stress.[6]

Data from the 1963 survey of the aged by the Social Security Administration show "that half of the nonwhite married couples aged 65 or older had a money income in 1962 totaling less than $1,960. This median represented two-thirds that of white couples. Among nonmarried persons—that is, persons widowed, divorced, or never married—median income of nonwhite persons was four-fifths that of the white population among men and three-fourths among women."[7]

The annual income survey for 1962 by the Bureau of Census indicated a median income for all nonwhite families of only half that found among white families. "For persons living alone or with nonrelatives—most of them nonmarried and nearly 40 percent aged 65 or older—the nonwhite group has a median income two-thirds that of white persons."[8]

The factors that contribute to the vicious cycle for Negroes are lower educational attainment, less occupational opportunity, and discrimination in hiring and firing. Low earnings and lack of additional sources of revenue further reduce the chances of self-support among the Negro aged. Even well-educated Negroes fare poorly in comparison with their white counterparts. "About a fourth of the couples and a sixth of the nonmarried persons received income in the form of interest, dividends, or rents. Among the white aged, two-thirds of the couples and about half of the nonmarried reported such income."[9]

Home ownership was minimal and condition of living arrangements inadequate according to the decennial census of 1960. "Among all white households with an aged head, 70 percent owned their home, compared with 54 percent of the nonwhite households. More than a fourth of the units rented by nonwhite households and almost a fifth of those owned were described as dilapidated . . . Among the white households headed by an aged person, only 3 percent of them owned units and 6 percent of those rented were classed as dilapidated."[10]

It is Orshansky's contention, however, that through social security and old-age assistance programs, the Negro aged arrive at closer parity with the economic resources of the aged white population. She observes, "The income of the average white worker is more sharply reduced in retirement than the income of the Negro worker, thus drawing the two groups closer together in the common bond of stringency."[11] But she also notes that "the prelude to poverty in old age" begins much earlier and is modified in old age mainly because public assistance programs are geared to help at that point.[12]

The case of the Negro aged accentuates the economic conditions among far too many aged and reaffirms the principle that early preparation for aging would go far to alert persons to the inevitable economic tribulations of ill-prepared elders.

Political Activity

National concern over aging citizens has stirred federal, state, and local governments into initiating a variety of programs to prevent or ameliorate problems. A majority of these programs may be traced back to the time of the Great Depression, the

1930s. For the first time in American history, the government took positive and deliberate steps to cope with economic stress among the aged.

While there were many precedents prior to the 1935 enactment of the social security program, such as retirement benefit plans and homes for retired workers sponsored by major corporations and trade unions and state programs such as California's mandatory old-age assistance program of 1929, perhaps the urgency of the times was best dramatized by the popular appeal of the Townsend Plan, which proposed to place $200 a month in the hands of persons sixty years of age and older with the requirement that it be spent within the ensuing thirty days. Not only would the aged be elevated to a status of dignity, but the rapid circulation of money would stimulate the economy. Funding for this program would be derived from a modest "transaction tax" on purchases. Frequent changes or alterations were made in this basic scheme by its proponents, who resolutely supported their leader, Dr. Francis E. Townsend of Long Beach, California. While its economic soundness was frequently attacked, the plan's appeal amazed even its founders. At its zenith, the Townsend Plan was endorsed by some 2 million members enrolled in about 7,000 clubs.[13]

Those who are familiar with its impact credit the Townsend Plan's mass appeal as one of the catalytic agents that produced the Social Security Act of 1935. Repeatedly enlarged in coverage and scope, the Old-Age, Survivors, and Disability Insurance (OASDI), as it is properly called, holds the dominant position in income maintenance and attendant services for older persons in the nation.

OASDI is financed by a tax on earnings, currently up to a $6,600 ceiling, with both employee and employer making an equal contribution. The percentage of contributions is scheduled for graduated increases to 1987 but can be amended by Congress. Qualifications for benefits are based on length of covered employment based upon date of birth or, if a worker dies or is disabled, the date of this event. A person is fully covered if he has one-quarter year of coverage for every year after 1950, up to but not including the year he reaches sixty-five (sixty-two for women), dies, or becomes disabled. Disability benefits are granted if a worker has credit for five out of ten years before the date of the disability. Blindness before age thirty-one can also qualify a worker with a briefer span of coverage. Men may retire at age sixty-two with a reduction in monthly benefits.

Married workers with children under eighteen at retirement receive additional benefits. Half the worker's benefits are granted to his wife even if she is under sixty-two, and half his benefits are granted for the underage children. Eventually, the maximum family benefit is $368 per month under present law. Ordinarily, benefits for children stop at age eighteen unless a child has been permanently and totally disabled before that age. A recent amendment provides for continued benefits if dependent children up to twenty-two are attending school full time. In addition, survivor benefits include a lump-sum payment for burial expenses up to $255 for the insured worker; benefits for dependent children until age eighteen or until twenty-two if they attend school full time; widow's benefits while she has children in her care, which are resumed at age sixty or sixty-two unless she has remarried; and benefits for dependent parents aged sixty-two or more if they were receiving at least half their support from the worker prior to his death and if they are not receiving old age benefits from their own earnings. With over 600 district offices throughout the country and seven major pay centers, the Social Security Administration is charged with a tremendously complicated responsibility.

Amendments in 1965 added to the technical tasks of the social security system. These provided for hospital insurance and for voluntary medical insurance, popularly known as Medicare. As of July, 1966, the hospital insurance program covered the cost of up to sixty days in a hospital, less $40 deductible, and all but $10 a day for an additional thirty days in each "spell of illness." As of January 1, 1967, costs for up to twenty days in an extended-care facility, which includes qualified nursing homes and convalescent hospital sections, will be paid, and all but $5 a day for an additional eighty days for each spell of illness. At least three days of hospitalization must precede extended care. Further, up to 100 home visits by nurses or other health workers in the year following release from hospital or extended-care facility and 80 percent of the cost, after the first $20 deductible, for out-patient diagnostic tests for each twenty-day period of testing will be paid.

The medical-insurance program requires an aged person to register voluntarily for it and to pay $3 a month, which is matched by another $3 from the federal government. Some 80 percent of the reasonable charges, with the first $50 deductible, may be paid in each calendar year for physicians' and surgeons' services; for home health services, even without a hospital stay, up to 100 visits per year; and for other treatments such as needed for diagnoses, dressings, splints, and rental equipment.

This particular program has been one of the most controversial issues in the United States and has been resisted for years by many medical practitioners through their representative organizations. Cooperation between members of the medical profession and authorized administrators of the medical-insurance program is essential and calls for diplomacy in the light of past resistance. The fear of government intervention in professional enterprise appears to be very real for medical personnel. On the other hand, the need for documentation of services rendered before payment can be authorized is paramount in the operation of a government agency. That former professional freedoms can be inviolate when red tape is involved is questionable. But there is need to remember that the rising costs of health care for the aged have brought the program into existence, and alternate proposals to date have been politically defeated.

Old Age Assistance (OAA) is supplementary to the Social Security Act and provides for a federal grants-in-aid program for states providing for their own needy aged, especially the aged who do not qualify for insurance benefits or who have special needs. The federal government shares in the cost of state programs for the indigent aged up to a current maximum of $75. The first $37 of the payment is covered by the federal government in a ratio of 31 to 37. The remaining $38 is also covered by the federal government, but will vary according to a state's per capita income from 50 to 65 percent. Additional federal assistance is provided for medical care for the aged and other services for the blind and disabled.

The Older Americans Act of 1965 is one of the most recent efforts to further expand government services for the aged. The Administration on Aging, headed by a commissioner appointed by the President, is authorized to become a clearinghouse for information relating to the problems of the aged and aging; to administer all grants provided in the act; to develop, conduct, and arrange for research and demonstration programs on aging; to provide technical assistance and consultation services to states and to other government agencies; to prepare, publish, and disseminate educational materials dealing with the welfare of older persons; to gather statistics on aging not available through other federal agencies; and to encourage effective use of current resources and available services for the aged and aging.

These major programs, without further reference to other established programs, represent a political response to the expressed needs of the aged and lend tremendous political support for gerontological investigation. Objectively, they are also products of the transfer of functions that were formerly the exclusive province of other social institutions.

Family and Aging

Families normally serve throughout the aging process, from the infant's cries for help, through the dependent and formative years of childhood and adolescence, to the final moments when life ebbs away. Failure of the family to serve as a primary refuge from sociopsychological threats may force a person to seek substitutes, which may or may not protect the vulnerable. Indeed, most painful of all, families may be the cause of personality difficulties. Aging accentuates whatever family strengths or weaknesses may exist.

A familiar retirement syndrome consists of a husband returning to his home and spending his full time with his spouse. His wife generally cannot retire from her domestic tasks and finds her routine disrupted by the presence of her husband. Especially if their children are absent, whatever ties that bind them together are sorely tested. Family conflicts of long standing may now take center stage.[14]

According to the most recent data available from the U.S. Bureau of the Census, the vast majority of older men and women in the United States in 1965 lived in such husband-wife households—namely, 5,287,000, or 66.8 percent, of the men and 3,389,000, or 33.3 percent, of the women. Only 1 in 25 lived in an institution—namely, 277,000, or 3.5 percent, of the men and 440,000, or 4.3 percent, of the women. Some 1,283,000, or 16.2 percent, of the men lived alone or with nonrelatives, and 3,329,000, or 32.7 percent, of the women had similar arrangements. Living with a relative were some 712,000, or 9.4 percent, of the men and some 1,918,000, or 18.9 percent, of the women. The men continuing as family head but without their spouse numbered 351,000, or 4.4 percent. Women as family head, without their spouse, numbered 1,091,000, or 10.7 percent. These data suggest that the retirement syndrome described above is indeed present for vast numbers of aged persons. Demographic data already cited further indicate that the final stage of family life, sometimes called the stage of the empty nest or the family of gerontation, will occur with even greater frequency in the future.

The possibility of conflict-ridden situations, however, does not deter older persons from remaining married or reentering matrimony. In the United States in 1965, most older men were married—namely, 71.3 percent of their numbers and 36 percent of the older women. In 1965, some 54.4 percent of older women were widowed; their ratio to widowers is 4 to 1. In addition, some 35,000 marriages occur annually in the United States in which the groom, the bride, or both are sixty-five or older. These older marriages are currently increasing.

An arrangement of special interest to social gerontologists is the three-generation family household, in which a "middle generation" married couple, their children, and one or more of their aged parents live under the same roof.[15] The most typical pattern appears to be one of an older woman, usually the mother of the wife, living with her daughter, her son-in-law, and their children. Optimum conditions consist of insightful flexibility on the part of the middle generation to satisfy the needs of both their parents and their children. Departure from this pattern initiates painful dilemmas that vary from mild disagreements to open familial warfare.

Role reversal in a family appears to be one of the most difficult changes older persons face. An "independent" parent becomes a "dependent" child, or a formerly "dependent" child assumes the prerogatives of an "independent" parent. The transmission of power is charged with possibilities for "revenge" for real or imagined wrongs, for "rewards" for past debts, for "resistance" to loss of authority, and for "resignation" to the loss of freedom.[16]

Postparental life, of course, brings considerable pleasure to many older persons.[17] Being a grandparent can confer some degree of privilege not accorded a parent. David and Vera Mace have described the Russian grandmother, the *babushka*, as one of the most helpful figures in Soviet families.[18] Whether the *babushka* role is appropriate to American conditions, however, remains one of the many unanswered questions concerning the aged in the family institution.

Education and the Aging

The skeptical question whether or not older persons have the capacity to continue learning with any great chance of success. Charles Cohen has examined research on the ability of the aged to learn and finds, contrary to much folklore, that "if there is a decrement at all, it is not large enough to be significant."[19] He concludes: "(1) Successful learning is possible past 60. (2) Learning situations must take into account physiological abilities of older adults. (3) Attitudes and motivations need to be taken into account. In brief, educational areas must be relevant to older persons."[20]

David Moberg has suggested that, if new educational programs among the aged are to be developed, the following objectives would prove appropriate: (1) service to others; (2) independent mind and action; (3) sense of humor cultivated; (4) cultivation of appreciation of fine arts; (5) time and opportunity to be creative; and (6) mental alertness to be cultivated.[21]

It is apparent that educators are receptive to programs designed to educate the aged because they take an optimistic view of the potential of older persons. The stereotypic notion that intellectual curiosity is solely the possession of younger persons is challenged by those who have taken the time to incorporate older persons into a scholarly environment and have noted the enthusiastic responses. A number of programs have been well received, such as those at the University of Rhode Island[22] and Port Charlotte, Florida.[23] For those who wish to make up educational deprivations, much can be done. In 1966, 373,338 persons over eighteen who had completed less than six grades of school were attending basic education classes in all fifty states under the Economic Opportunity Act of 1964.[24] While improved economic status was the paramount objective of most of these persons, many attended solely for intrinsic educational values.

Educators have known for years that ability is ageless. Older persons, especially in a university setting, have much to gain in returning to a campus. Younger generations profit by their presence and experience. Provisos, of course, are in order because neither educators nor students of any age are totally suited for educational situations. For the well motivated, however, continued exploration of knowledge is a feasible prospect. Perhaps well-designed communities of elders in the future will include schools and universities as a matter of course, just as they currently include benches, shuffleboard courts, golf courses, or pleasant vistas.

Summation

The presence of large numbers of older persons has been felt by the major social institutions. Appropriate adjustments are needed, but consensus as to what constitutes "appropriate adjustments" has not yet been reached. Religious organizations have been moderately successful in including older persons in their activities. However, as a resource effective in meeting personal or social needs, religion has been found wanting. In a generally prosperous economy, the vast majority of aged continues to be excluded. Political leadership has attempted to close the gap between necessary economic and social support and economic deprivation.

Youth orientation is evident in the family and in education. Both, however, show signs of awakening to the full import of gerontation. The growing mood of receptivity must now be matched with demonstrably effective structures and procedures that will build upon the still untapped strengths of the aged.

CHAPTER *NINE*

Research and Social Gerontology

The basic business of social gerontology is to develop empiric evidence concerning the aging process, its effects upon individuals, and ultimately its effects upon social systems. There is no doubt that social gerontologists take their responsibilities very seriously and, judging from the mountains of data they have accumulated over the years, have conscientiously attended to their research-oriented task. Indeed, like so many other specialists, the professional social gerontologist is frequently hard pressed to keep up with the latest studies, issues, conferences, and shifts in theoretical conceptions.

No one person can be said to command all available knowledge on aging, but there are nationally known and internationally known scholars whose years of experience, perseverance, and dedication have earned them the esteem of those who have more recently selected social gerontology as a major interest. These "founding fathers" are still actively contributing their leadership, particularly in the United States, because of the relative youthfulness of the field. The passing of such inspirational models as Ernest W. Burgess and Robert W. Kleemeir is sorely regretted.

If experience in research work itself has taught any lessons of merit, perhaps one of the most important is *patience*. Youth tends to be more impetuous, impatient with developments, especially scientific growth. Questions on aging need answering and problems need resolution, but they do not come overnight in swift, giant strides. Research studies probably will continue to be painstaking, cautious, and exploratory, and its conclusions tentative and conditional. Scientific research and theory, after all, consist of organized, systemized trial and error. Data may accumulate rather convincingly in one direction, suggesting that evidence is overwhelming in support of one theory, but all this can be quickly reversed or invalidated if the conclusions are found to be products of unconscious bias or methodological selectivity. Findings based on only institutionalized aged instead of healthy, noninstitutionalized aged is a case in point.

Empiric work is apparently not immune to human folly, fancy, or fashion despite its avowed dedication to objectivity, its effort at maximum depersonalization, and its unremitting pursuit of validity.[1] Perfection in technique, methodology, and theory is desirable, but most research effort settles for something short of this ideal. These rather general observations, of course, have much significance for future investigations in social gerontology. The very topic of aging and the aged makes definitive work in the field pressing because the research distillations are of immediate concern to those who have precious little time.

Practical Nature of Gerontological Research

In much of what passes for gerontological study, there is a curious mixture of the practical—the applied or geriatric—research, coupled with pure, basic, or fundamental research that purports to be disinterested in immediate applications. The goal of many social gerontologists appears to be service to the aged rather than unhurried and dispassionate analyses and syntheses of gerontological knowledge. The foregoing is not intended as criticism, for it is understandable in the light of the history of the science of aging, which had its origins in practical and constructive help for older persons.

There appears to be a definite pattern in the history of services on behalf of the "needy" that applies equally well to social gerontology. Generally, some astute and sensitive persons and organizations become aware of society's failure to incorporate certain segments into mutually acceptable statuses and roles. The needs of these segments often originate in the unplanned consequences of social change. The needs of the minority in terms of power, for example, may continue to be ignored for prolonged periods provided the majority is not discomforted. However, when the power gap becomes unbearable to the unprivileged and the privileged, the position of the privileged becomes tenuous and can be affected adversely by the presence of the deprived. Then the aroused minority captures attention, and active programs may be initiated. Examples of this pattern would be the cases for Negroes, women, children, the mentally ill, criminals, migrants, the unemployed, religious sects, and the poor. The aged constitute a more recent entrant in this paradigm.

Social service programs intended to bring the needy into balance with the ongoing society may be of a variety of types based on a variety of indexes. They may be minimal or maximal, resisted or encouraged, ameliorative or ineffective shifts in social policy, sporadic or continuous, isolated or organized into a common plan, disintegrative or integrative, and treated as burdensome side issues or as responsibilities and main issues. The latter end of each of these indexes seems to apply to social service programs for the aged in America.

The accomplishments of social service programs for the aged are subject to intensive investigation. The sums of money invested in the programs from both private and public funds are great. If the various agencies and their programs are doing what they set out to do, then positive findings are expected. If evidence indicates inept management and minimal effects, then the programs may lose their financial support. Social service agencies are becoming increasingly aware that research is an adjunct of their work and so have opened a new field for capable, research-oriented personnel.[2]

Definition of Terms in Social Gerontology

One of the characteristics of scientific investigation is precision. The units of measurement, the topics under investigation, or the areas of inquiry must not be so ambiguous, vague, or all-inclusive as to nullify their usefulness. What, for example, is the meaning of "retirement"? Is it an act or a condition?[3] Is a person "retired" when he has reached a specified age and has been so declared by his employers, despite his continued employment, albeit with a reduced or even increased work load? Is a person "retired" if he leaves one type of employment but enters a second career in his later years? Is a person "retired" when he no longer receives wages or a salary, but pursues such work as consultations, speaking engagements, executive decisions, and writing for influential publications? Social gerontologists have not reached consensus on the term "retired" despite its central position in gerontological literature. Behavioral sciences have depended on operational definitions, terms derived from specified procedures.

Like all new entrants into the sciences, social gerontology stands in need of clarity of terms, concepts, and other abstractions. The technical jargon used by the "initiated" limits common discourse. "Social space," "poverty," "disengagement," "isolation," and "aging" have specific cognitive content, for example, to social gerontologists. Refinement of terms will continue for some time.

Carlos Reed has recently suggested that the nomenclature of aging be substantially revised to avoid confusion, error, and subjective preferences.[4] Even the pronunciation of the term "geriatrics" is a departure from the pronunciation of the original Greek *geras* ("old"); it should be "geriatrics," not "jeriatrics" as it is in common usage.[5] Aside from its pronunciation, Reed accepts "geriatrics" because of its specificity, but suggests, among other possibilities, the substitution of the following terms: "geratage" to replace "gerontage"; "geratize" to replace "age" as a verb, along with all derivatives; "geratology" to replace "gerontology"; "gerist" to replace "geron," "geront," "retiree," and "senior citizen."[6]

There is disparagement of women, who constitute the vast majority of older persons, by the current use of the root *geron*, which is the Greek term for "old man." The feminine counterpart of *geron* is *graus*, which means "old woman"; but because the term does not lend itself to euphonious designation, Reed urges the acceptance of the neologism "gerist," as applied to an older person of either sex.[7]

The arguments favoring these changes seem reasonable enough and are clearly motivated by a desire to serve objectivity. These suggestions may or may not be generally adopted in the literature, but they represent the serious efforts of gerontologists to improve communication for specialists entering the field from a variety of disciplines.

Assessment of Selected Aging Research[8]

Social gerontology is concerned with the problem of "facilitating the social functioning of the aged in the face of health impairments."[9] A recent study by three panels of sixty experts each in health administration, sociology, and medicine has been made of 250 projects concerned with health in the United States between 1954 and 1960. Their work provides possible guidelines for future research policy on aging.

Of the 250 projects, 70 dealt directly with the health and functioning of the aged and were rated by each panel as twice as important as any other health problem facing the nation. Administrators, understandably, rated research in terms of problem solution, whereas sociologists evaluated studies for their long-range significance. Physicians took a middle position in rating research efforts because they could understand the administrators' concern for immediate practical help and yet could sympathize with the "go slow" policy of sociologists, who were more interested in building sound theory. These differences between the panels take on added meaning if team research is to be ultimately developed among representatives of all three disciplines. Failure to understand each other's needs could mean a decline in research activity.

Gerald Gordon of the Graduate School of Business at the University of Chicago has suggested five levels of research activities in an attempt to systematize problem-oriented studies:

1. *Delineation of the problem:* Measures of the extent and importance of a problem.
2. *Causal relationships:* Determination of those factors which promote or inhibit the existence of the problem.
3. *Factors related to the problem solution:* Determination of the technical and social factors affecting the implementation of procedures to solve a given problem.
4. *Problem solution:* Development and testing of a given program aimed at the amelioration of the problem. The solution may be behavioral, technical, or both.
5. *Evaluation:* The controlled evaluation of a specific action program.[10]

Gordon finds that most research on the aged has generally been confined to the first three levels and that relatively few studies have concentrated on the last two levels.

It is instructive to cite ten lines of gerontological study that all three panels found most important, not by reason of the research quality or the significance of their findings, but by reason of the problem to which each study is addressed. The leading ten studies, stating their purposes as closely as possible, are:

1. To determine relationships between selected medical, sociological, and psychological variables and coronary arteriosclerosis.
2. To describe and identify significant social variables associated with health, employment, and familial and associational status of the "normal" aging population.
3. To determine the prevalence of chronic disease and to estimate the amount and kind of disability, rehabilitative potential, and needs for care in a rural population. To compare

household interviews, clinical examinations, and other methods of estimating prevalence of chronic disease.

4. First, to conduct field surveys in order to study the health needs and problems of the aged, their health, and social adjustments, the degree to which they require and utilize medical and social service available in the community and, second, to evaluate the functioning and effectiveness of the pilot program that was developed on the basis of information obtained during the field study.
5. To design a long-term study of hypertension that would serve to add to present knowledge about the natural history of the disorder.
6. To develop a methodology for the evaluation of patient care. The long-run basis of such a methodology is a task-resource model that is being developed to relate the physical, social, psychological, and economic dimensions of the hospital to the tasks performed in providing patient care. The major resource dimensions are taken to be the practice of medicine and supporting tasks of selection, service, supply, and control.
7. To investigate the effect of man's adaptation to his environment, especially his social environment, upon his health.
8. To determine, first, the extent of accurate knowledge, as well as misinformation, about cancer, its symptoms, diagnosis, prevention, treatment, and resources available for care; second, sources of knowledge; third, the role of the American Cancer Society as a source of effective knowledge. Finally, to recommend procedures to motivate the "hard-to-reach" group.
9. To discover if chronic, recurring stress is a factor in coronary heart disease and what the social and personality correlates of coronary heart disease are.
10. To identify the characteristics of patients receiving long-term nursing care in institutions by sex, age, marital status, and diagnosis and to survey the nursing care received by these patients.[11]

Aging research has thus attempted to come to grips with puzzling problems and has been receiving increasing support and encouragement. Nevertheless, research strategy requires concentration on gaps in the knowledge that remain. Central to gerontological research is the relation between aging individuals and society. Overall nexuses have yet to be fully substantiated. A society's ability to incorporate all age grades into its structure in a mutually satisfying pattern is paramount in this connection. When specific studies are warranted, they should be in the area of dealing effectively with potential health problems of the aged.

Theory and Research

The action proneness that characterizes much gerontological study has troubled those who are keenly aware of the need for organized frameworks and perspectives to guide research efforts. The division of labor between researchers and theorists is a legitimate one, but enthusiasm and heavy investment for one side or the other have polarized scientists in many disciplines, including social gerontology. This is a familiar "battleground" to graduate students who are the latest recruits in scientific skirmishes. Depending upon early undergraduate propensities, bias of graduate mentors, and the student's own personality, university trainees take sides despite elaborate precaution that research and theory are indispensable to each other and one must cultivate an appreciation for the relevance of both.

Social gerontology has developed comparatively little theory since its inception. The abundance of research on aging is mute testimony to where the emphasis has been placed. Perhaps a portion of this lopsided picture is due to the need to "get moving" in view of the long neglect of the aged. Another possible explanation is the assumption that current theory in such related fields as psychology, sociology, economics, political science, and biology is adequate for gerontological purposes. Still another possibility is the stronger interest in humanistic or nonscientific concerns, a point that merits greater attention. Finally, a number of specialists are so enamored of their own considerable skills and insights that they are relatively alienated from the overall gerontological context to which they are tied. Hans Zetterberg notes, "The use of mathematics is . . . an escape from the well-tested inability of many sociologists to write an attractive, literary prose."[12] He is, of course, not opposed to mathematical precision, but suggests a compromise for "a very disciplined ordinary language in theoretical sociology occasionally supported by mathematical expressions and graphs."[13]

In a significant conclusion, Zetterberg comments on the relation between research and theory in sociology. It is strikingly similar to the needs of social gerontology in this respect.

Most problems for social research at present are not suggested by theoretical sociology. They are suggested by the whim or wisdom of foundation officials; by clients who want sociological help to acquire a larger share of markets, commodities or votes; by journalists, clergymen, and others who choose to debate certain issues of the day as social problems. The typical sociological research project is an *ad hoc* study of topics suggested by non-sociologists. It is sheer accident when these topics can be integrated in sociological theory. The studies of these topics, accordingly, face difficult problems of verification. Moreover, they are not cumulative; the best that can be said for them is that they foster methodological advances.

By contrast, the studies suggested by existing theory are cumulative, and their problems of verification are modest. This state of affairs, when a theory guides the choice of research topics, is "normal science," and it prevails until research findings no longer seem in regular agreement with the postulates of the theory and alternatives are formulated. At such a point, it no longer suffices to merely amend and elaborate the theory; the scientific community goes through a "revolution" and the Young Turks emerge with a novel theory, which serves as a guide to novel research topics. Such has been the pattern of most sciences.[14]

Engagement and Disengagement Theories

The work of Elaine Cumming and her associates has been noted earlier. Their functionalist theory of aging is presented and tested in *Growing Old*.[15] The disengagement theory presented therein challenges engagement theory and has provoked healthy disagreement among social gerontologists. Arnold Rose has carefully examined disengagement theory and clarifies its nature by pointing out what it does *not* state as well as what it *does* state.[16] He notes:

1. It is *not* a hypothesis which states that, as people get older, they are gradually separated from their associations and their social functions. This is an assumed fact.
2. It does *not* state that "as people become physically feebler or chronically ill, they are thereby forced to abandon their associations and social functions." Persons in poor physical or mental health were excluded from their sample and thus the disengagement theory does not rest upon ill health.
3. It "does *not* say that because older people tend to have a reduced income in our society, they can no longer afford to participate in many things." This is also logic and a fact. Those with limited funds were also excluded in the sample of Cumming and Henry.

   What the disengagement theory *does* say is that "the society and the individual prepare *in advance* for the ultimate disengagement of incurable, incapacitating disease and death by an *inevitable, gradual, and mutually satisfying process of disengagement.*" By this means, both society and individuals are not disturbed or disrupted because society may continue its structures and functions and individuals may leave, satisfied that their departure does not disturb those associations with which they were once connected.[17]

Modifying her theory to add greater "rigor," Cumming noted that the original study "did not take into account such non-modal cases as widowhood before the marriage of the last child or of work protracted past the modal year of retirement."[18]

Some individual differences were acknowledged as "typologies of withdrawal and retreat" and might involve cases of reengagement. Polar types would be "the impinger" and "the selector."[19]

The impinger is more an activist who "tries out" his concept of himself in interaction with others; he uses their appropriate responses to confirm the correctness of his inferences about himself, the environment and his relationship to it. If the feedback from others suggests that he is incorrect, the impinger will try to bring others' responses into line with his own sense of appropriate relationship. Only if he fails repeatedly will he modify his concept of himself.

. . .

The selector, however, tends to wait for others to affirm his assumptions about himself. From the ongoing flow of stimulation he selects those cues that confirm his relationship to the world. If they fail to come, he waits, and only reluctantly brings his own concepts into line with the feedback he is getting.[20]

Between the two, although there are mixed types, the impinger can be expected to suffer more distress than a selector in the early stages of disengagement.[21]

Three lines of criticism suggest that the disengagement theory may not be correct. The first questions the theory for *all* persons and accepts it, in part, only as a life style for *some* people.[22] The second does not accept the value judgment that disengagement is desirable for older people.[23] The third objection is that the theory does not fit the facts concerning social structures and trends.[24]

As Rose notes, those who have disengaged have been forced into such a position by such pressures as youth orientation, compulsory retirement, and minimal opportunities in self-employment. None of these is irreversible. In fact, modern medicine and health measures have reduced the desire to disengage because an increasing number of persons sixty-five and older are in good health and are vigorous in body and mind. Public and private pension and annuity plans are removing economic impediments to continued social engagement. There is strong movement toward improvement of the status of the aged by leadership among the aged themselves. Finally, the earlier disengagement of men from work and women from childbearing suggests that men and women are free to reengage themselves in a variety of roles, such as in voluntary associations and gainful employment, with less pressure or fear of failure as in earlier years.

Those who endorse the engagement theory have won strong support for action programs to provide for and prolong firm bonds between aging individuals and their society. Those who favor disengagement insist that the bonds between aging individuals and their social milieu must inevitably be reduced and finally severed. The latter perspective has not as many advocates as the former. The "adding life to the years" and "retirement to life" slogans make good sense in terms of sociopsychological well-being. Study after study reports positive results in terms of good health and continued services by the elderly. On the other hand, "growing old gracefully" implies to some a shifting to a new, rather threatening status of being shelved, sidelined, and side-stepped. Recognition of limitations imposed by the aging process, also well documented by numerous studies, leads to the "roleless role" of the aged, which may be filled with attractions of its own. Research in these matters has barely begun, but knowledge is accumulating.

The Nature of Aging

The facile acceptance of physical aging as a process of normal "wear and tear" or increasing decrements has been challenged by a newer view that aging can be treated as a "disease" whose effects can be reduced and possibly reversed.

Psychologists have done much to delineate "life styles," which vary in their adaptability to the triumphs and tribulations of life. Sociologists, economists, and political scientists have analyzed the ability or inability of social structures to handle the increasing number and proportion of older persons. In this presentation, society has been viewed as an "enabling" or a "disabling" agency for the aged. At one extreme, it can find "social space" for all age grades and, at the other, it can treat older age grades as obsolete and as discards to be shed as quickly as possible.

Some analysts consider the aged a "minority" who can disrupt the lives of the majority who are in mid-life. Arnold Rose merits special attention for his objective description of the aged as a "subculture" growing increasingly "age-group conscious."[25]

Research is continuing along all these lines and gives promise of a much brighter future for the aged than has heretofore been possible.

Humanism and Scientism

A binding thread running through the entire field of social gerontology is an abiding concern for human life. It is admittedly an idealistic and sentimental concern, but undoubtedly it inspires and sustains the prosaic and mundane tasks required to deal effectively with the elderly. Although scientists divest themselves of emotionalism and mystical biases, buried deep in their consciousness is a faith that what they do is worthy and ultimately for the good of mankind. In their public lectures and publications and in their private conversations and deeds, they espouse causes and viewpoints in the context of their work with a fervor that would do credit to a persuasive divine.

One of the most eloquent spokesmen for humanism, that is, the evaluation that human beings are endowed with divine spirit, is Dr. Abraham J. Heschel, Professor of Jewish Ethics and Mysticism at the Jewish Theological Seminary in New York. Dr. Heschel presented a paper before a special session of the 1961 White House Conference on Aging that provoked unprecedented acclaim.[26] Excerpts from his address illustrate the humanistic philosophy that underlies much of social gerontology:

> The test of a people is how it behaves toward the old. It is easy to love children. Even tyrants and dictators make a point of being fond of children. But the affection and care for the old, the incurable, the helpless, are the true gold mines of a people.[27]
>
> . . .
>
> The tragedy is that old age comes upon us as a shock for which we are unprepared. If life is defined exclusively in terms of functions

and activities, is it still worth living when these functions and activities are sharply curtailed?[28]

. . .

The years of old age may enable us to attain the high values we failed to sense, the insights we have missed, the wisdom we ignored. They are indeed formative years, rich in possibilities, to unlearn the follies of a lifetime, to see through inbred self-deceptions, to deepen understanding and compassion, to widen the horizon of honesty, to refine the sense of fairness.

One ought to enter old age the way one enters the senior year at a university, in exciting anticipation of consummation, of the summing-up.[29]

. . .

Old age has the vicious tendency of depriving a person of the present. The aged thinks of himself as belonging to the past. But it is precisely the openness to the present that he must strive for.

He who lives with a sense for the Presence knows that to get older does not mean to lose time but rather to gain time. And he also knows that in all his deeds, the chief task of man is *to sanctify time*. All it takes to sanctify time is God, a soul, and a moment. And the three are always here . . . Just to be is a blessing, just to live is holy.[30]

Just as eloquent a spokesman for scientism was George Lundberg of the University of Washington. Faith that the diligent use of scientific methods and attitudes could markedly improve human conditions runs through his classic *Can Science Save Us?*[31] Lundberg warned that scientists should not attempt to assume too much for their work. He wrote:

Indeed, nothing that I have said regarding the possibilities of scientific study of human affairs should be interpreted as in any way contemplating an abandonment or a restriction upon the artistic, religious, literary, or recreational arts which also minister to the cravings of men. I have on the contrary rather advocated that the social sciences should not handicap themselves by aggrandizing to themselves roles which they cannot fulfill.[32]

What social scientists, including social gerontologists, can do was outlined by Lundberg:

Social scientists, as scientists, had better confine themselves to three tasks: First and foremost, they should devote themselves to developing reliable knowledge of what alternatives of action exist under given conditions and the probable consequences of each. Secondly, social scientists should, as a legitimate part of their technology as well as for its practical uses, be able to gauge reliably what the masses of men want under given circumstances. Finally, they should, in the applied aspects of their science, develop the administrative or engineering techniques of satisfying most efficiently and economically these wants, regardless of what they may be at a given time, regardless of how they may change from time to time, and regardless of the scientists' own preferences.[33]

The trust that Lundberg had, that "the masses of men" would "want" those things and conditions that would ennoble human life rather than degrade it, is evident. Otherwise, science becomes a voiceless tool that slavishly follows human whimsy "regardless" of what seem to be the prevailing values. Lundberg was correct when he argued for a value-free scientism, but the selection of scientific inquiries and the ultimate interpretation and use of findings require scientists to confront the realities of human organization. Humanism and scientism are thus intimately related in such fields as social gerontology, and many of its problems can be explained by the dilemmas that their joint presence imposes.

Research Problems in Social Gerontology

In empiric investigations, social gerontology shares many problems with other behavioral sciences. One problem is finding the appropriate balance between "pure" research, which seeks answers to fundamental questions without preconceptions that the answers have any pragmatic value, and "applied" research, which has immediate, practical uses. One must judge for himself whether the biological or the social sciences have done more basic research.[34]

Another common research problem is determining the relative merits of cross-sectional and longitudinal studies. Out of economic and administrative necessity, most social gerontologists have produced cross-sectional studies rather than longitudinal ones. However, increased funding of gerontological projects promises to reverse this imbalance in the future.

Certainly representative sampling has always been one of the most meaningful methods in research. In the study of aging, much effort has been expended toward sampling the less-available world of the well-aged, perhaps the more important majority of the aged, rather than the captive, available, institutionalized aged. This augurs well for social gerontological study.

American gerontologists are quite aware of the culture-bound nature of their work. Cross-cultural comparisons, however, have not been forgotten from the earliest beginnings of social gerontological study, such as Simmons' classic work on preindustrial societies, Burgess' on Western industrialized societies, and the periodic international gerontological congresses. The universality of aging suggests that further work among all nations and cultures will continue and will be encouraged.

There is always room for creativity and innovation in gerontological research. Replication, almost *ad nauseam*, follows every successful research effort. Some duplication and repetition are justifiable in learning, substantiation, or continued verification, but there is a point of diminishing returns even for gigantic efforts. There is a standing invitation among the scientifically inquisitive to those willing to strike out in new directions. For the young scholar who is fortified by familiarity with past achievements but who is not rigid, social gerontology is a fertile specialization.

The more unique research problems of social gerontology include (1) the difficulty of working with recalcitrant aged who self-hate or who deny association with the elderly, (2) the development of age-appropriate techniques to reach the aged, (3) the overcoming of inertia and time-hardened notions that defy tampering or alteration, (4) developing the delicacy and tact essential to rapport with older persons who are more alienated from the present and future than the investigators, (5) the possibility of damaging whatever tenuous ties the elderly may have with others, and (6) finding intergeneration values that transcend age.

Summation

The *raison d'être* of social gerontology is to help the aged through its research and theory. In the zeal to "do good" for the aged, much gerontological study and thinking have been pragmatic or essentially geriatric. There is no serious quarrel with this practical emphasis except for the imbalance that ensues. Justifying expenditure of large sums may sidetrack the pressing need to provide basic knowledge before intelligent action programs can be established. Even in basic terms, much work remains toward providing the means for common discourse.

Problem orientation, then, characterizes gerontological research, particularly in the area of health needs of the aged. This emphasis has produced mountains of research and molehills of theory. Social gerontology's future as a specialized discipline depends heavily upon the freeing of inquiry to develop cumulative, nomothetic propositions. To date, the engagement theory versus the disengagement theory has occupied attention. Perhaps an intelligent admixture of both themes may contain the resolution of dilemmas confronting all persons.

A part of the difficulty impeding the progress of fundamental study of the aging is striking the appropriate balance between humanism and scientism. Spokesmen of the former eloquently plead for the sacred nature of all human beings. Scientists call for dispassionate evaluation of alternatives of action. Perhaps the first can supply the motivation for involvement and the second can furnish the essential knowledge to accomplish desired ends. Research problems in social gerontology are similar to those in all scientific fields, but circumstances peculiar to the aging process and the aged call for innovators willing to apply themselves to a major emerging scientific specialty.

NOTES

CHAPTER ONE

1. See, for example, Bernard Berelson and Gary A. Steiner, *Human Behavior: An Inventory of Scientific Findings* (New York: Harcourt, Brace & World, 1964).

2. For elaboration on this point, see Robert Fulton (ed.), *Death and Identity* (New York: Wiley, 1965).

3. See Leo W. Simmons, "Aging in Pre-Industrial Cultures," in Clark Tibbitts and Wilma Donahue (eds.), *Aging in Today's Society* (Englewood Cliffs, N.J.: Prentice-Hall, 1960), pp. 65–103.

4. For a fuller and more detailed statistical analysis of the demographic profile of aging and the aged, see Paul H. Jacobson, "Cohort Survival for Generations Since 1840," *The Milbank Memorial Fund Quarterly*, Vol. XLII, No. 3 (July, 1964), Part I.

5. Edmund V. Cowdry, *Problems of Ageing* (Baltimore: Williams & Wilkins, 1939).

6. Leo W. Simmons, *The Role of the Aged in Primitive Society* (New Haven: Yale University Press, 1945).

7. Otto Pollack, *Social Adjustment in Old Age* (New York: Social Science Research Council, 1948).

8. Ruth S. Cavan, *et al.*, *Personal Adjustment in Old Age* (Chicago: Science Research Associates, 1949).

9. The work of the Fifth International Congress in San Francisco has been summarized in two volumes: Nathan W. Shock (ed.), *Biological Aspects of Aging* (New York: Columbia University Press, 1962); and Jerome Kaplan and Gordon J. Aldridge (eds.), *Social Welfare of the Aging* (New York: Columbia University Press, 1962).

10. These were James E. Birren (ed.), *Handbook of Aging and the Individual* (Chicago: University of Chicago Press, 1959); Clark Tibbitts (ed.), *Handbook of Social Gerontology* (Chicago: University of Chicago Press, 1960); and Ernest W. Burgess (ed.), *Aging in Western Societies* (Chicago: University of Chicago Press, 1960).

11. See Michael Harrington, *The Other America* (New York: Macmillan, 1962).

12. See Marvin R. Koller, "Recommended Curricula in Social Gerontology," *Geriatrics*, XVII, No. 4 (April, 1962), 260–264.

13. I. Margulec, "The Care of the Aged in Israel," *The Gerontologist*, V, No. 2 (June, 1965), 61.

14. Burgess, *op. cit.*, p. 51.

15. *Ibid.*, p. 34.

16. See, for example, *Frauds and Deceptions Affecting the Elderly: Investigations, Findings, and Recommendations: 1964*, report of the Subcommittee on Frauds and Misrepresentations Affecting the Elderly to the Special Committee on Aging, United States Senate (Washington, D.C.: U.S. Government Printing Office, January 31, 1965).

17. See, for example, Hoke S. Simpson (ed.), *The Changing American Population* (New York: Institute of Life Insurance, 1962).

18. B. Kutner *et al.*, *Five Hundred Over Sixty* (New York: Russell Sage Foundation, 1956).

19. Harvey C. Lehman, *Age and Achievement* (Princeton, N.J.: Princeton University Press, 1953).

20. See, for example, John A. Hostetler, *Amish Society* (Baltimore: Johns Hopkins, 1963).

21. See Irving L. Webber, "The Organized Social Life of the Retired: Two Florida Communities," *American Journal of Sociology*, LIX (January, 1954), 340–346; Robert J. Havighurst and Ruth Albrecht, *Older People* (New York: Longmans, Green, 1957); Fern Long and Clara Luciola, "The Live Long and Like It Club," *Wilson Library Bulletin*, XXIII (1948), 301–305; and Jere Hoar, "A Study of Free-Time Activities of 200 Aged Persons," *Sociology and Social Research*, XLV (January, 1961), 157–162. A major source for current developments among the aging is the monthly bulletin *Aging*, published by the Administration on Aging, U.S. Department of Health, Education, and Welfare, Washington, D.C.

22. Elaine Cumming, *et al.*, "Disengagement: A Tentative Theory of Aging," *Sociometry*, XXIII, No. 1 (1960), 23–35; and Elaine Cumming and William E. Henry, *Growing Old* (New York: Basic Books, 1961).

23. Elaine Cumming, "New Thoughts on the Theory of Disengagement," in Robert Kastenbaum (ed.), *New Thoughts on Old Age* (New York: Springer, 1964), pp. 3–18.

24. Fred Cottrell, "The Technological and Societal Basis of Aging," in Tibbitts (ed.), *Handbook of Social Gerontology*, *op. cit.*, pp. 92–119.

25. Juanita Kreps (ed.), *Employment, Income, and Retirement Problems of the Aged* (Durham, N.C.: Duke University Press, 1963).

26. See Donald N. Michael, *Cybernation: The Silent Conquest* (Santa Barbara, Calif.: Fund for the Republic, 1962).

27. See *Aiding Older People, Programs and Resources in the Federal Government* (Washington, D.C.: Federal Council on Aging, May, 1958); and *The Older American* (Washington, D.C.: President's Council on Aging, May, 1963).

28. For example, the state of Iowa established the Permanent Commission on Aging, June 2, 1965. See also *Proceedings of the Third Annual Governor's Conference on Aging* (Albany: New York State Office for the Aging, May 1, 1964).

29. David O. Moberg, "Religiosity in Old Age," *The Gerontologist*, V, No. 2 (June, 1965), 78–87.

CHAPTER TWO

1. Donald Bogue, *The Population of the United States* (New York: Free Press, 1959), pp. 763–764.

2. *Demographic Yearbook, 1963*, 15th ed. (New York: United Nations, 1964), p. 3.

3. *Ibid.* Data concerning available census counts in the world adopted from pp. 4–5.

4. *Ibid.*, p. 11.

5. Herman B. Brotman, *Facts on Aging* (Washington, D.C.: Office of Aging, U.S. Department of Health, Education, and Welfare, June, 1965), No. 9, OA No. 409, p. 1.

6. See Henry Sheldon, *The Older Population of the United States* (New York: Wiley, 1958).

7. See Fred Cottrell, "The Technological and Societal Basis of Aging," in Clark Tibbitts (ed.), *Handbook of Social Gerontology* (Chicago: University of Chicago Press, 1960), pp. 92–119.

8. Bogue, *op. cit.*, p. 102.

9. *Ibid.*, pp. 102–103.

10. Leon H. Keyserling, *Progress or Poverty* (Washington, D.C.: Conference on Economic Progress, December, 1964).

11. *Ibid.*, p. 79.

12. *Ibid.*, p. 78.

13. *Housing for the Elderly*, A Report of the Subcommittee on Housing for the Elderly to the Special Committee on Aging, U.S. Senate (Washington, D.C.: U.S. Government Printing Office, 1962), p. 2.

14. *Ibid.*, p. 3.

15. *Ibid.*

16. See Marvin B. Sussman and Lee Burchinal, "Kin Family Network: Unheralded Structure in Current Conceptualizations of Family Functioning," *Marriage and Family Living*, XXIV, No. 3 (August, 1962), 231–240.

17. *Statistical Bulletin*, Metropolitan Life Insurance Company, XLVI (February, 1965), 1.

18. *Ibid.*, p. 3.

19. *Statistical Bulletin*, Metropolitan Life Insurance Company, XLVI (November, 1965), 1–2.

20. See *The Older American* (Washington, D.C.: President's Council on Aging, 1963), p. 43.

CHAPTER THREE

1. See Wilma Donahue, "Relationship of Age of Perceivers to Their Social Perceptions," *The Gerontologist*, V, No. 4 (December, 1965), 241–245, 276–277. Judgments of age-homogeneous retirement communities are discussed in terms of young and old observers.

2. See Wilma Donahue and Clark Tibbitts (eds.), *The New Frontiers of Aging* (Ann Arbor: University of Michigan Press, 1957), p. 130.

3. Vladimir Korenchevsky, in Geoffrey H. Bourne (ed.), *Physiological and Pathological Ageing* (New York: Hafner, 1961), p. 51.

4. *Ibid.*, p. 52.

5. *Ibid.*, pp. 52–53.

6. Probably one of the greatest sources summarizing the studies of psychological aging is the monumental work James E. Birren (ed.), *Handbook of Aging and the Individual* (Chicago: University of Chicago Press, 1959). Thereafter, *The Journal of Gerontology* and *The Gerontologist*, both published by the Gerontological Society of St. Louis, Missouri, offer studies and theoretical developments in the 1960s.

7. For a recent study, see William K. Caird, "Aging and Short-Term Memory," *Journal of Gerontology*, XXI, No. 2 (April, 1966), 295–299.

8. See Kingsley Davis, "The Sociology of Parent-Youth Conflict," *American Sociological Review*, V (August, 1940), 523–535.

9. See "Successful Aging," in Richard H. Williams, Clark Tibbitts, and Wilma Donahue (eds.), *Processes of Aging* (New York: Atherton, 1963), I, 299–320.

10. Suzanne Reichard, Florine Livson, and Paul G. Petersen, *Aging and Personality: A Study of Eighty-Seven Older Men*, a report in the study directed by the late Else Frenkel-Brunswick (New York: Wiley, 1962).

11. Richard Williams and Claudine Wirths, *Lives Through the Years: Styles of Life and Successful Aging* (New York: Atherton, 1965), p. 11.

12. Harvey C. Lehman, *Age and Achievement* (Princeton, N.J.: Princeton University Press, 1953).

13. Wayne Dennis, "Creative Productivity Between the Ages of 20 and 80 Years," *Journal of Gerontology*, XXI, No. 1 (January, 1966), 7.

14. *Ibid.*

CHAPTER FOUR

1. Leo W. Simmons, *The Role of the Aged in Primitive Society* (New Haven: Yale University Press, 1945).

2. *Ibid.*, p. 19.

3. Leviticus 19:32.

4. Proverbs 23:22.

5. Micah 6:8.

6. See Robert Flacèlière, *Daily Life in Greece at the Time of Pericles* (New York: Macmillan, 1965), p. 80.

7. J. P. Mahaffy, *Social Life in Greece from Homer to Menander* (London: Macmillan, 1913), pp. 20–43.

8. Charles Burton Gulick, *The Life of the Ancient Greeks* (New York: Appleton, 1902), pp. 284–285.

9. From *Private Life of the Romans* by Harold W. Johnston. Copyright © 1903 by Scott, Foresman and Co.

10. Maria S. Haynes, "The Supposedly Golden Age for the Aged in Ancient Rome (A Study of Literary Concept of Old Age)," *The Gerontologist*, III, No. 1 (March, 1963), 26–35.

11. Excerpted from Brian Tierney, *Medieval Poor Law: A Sketch of Canonical Theory and Its Application in England* (Berkeley and Los Angeles: University of California Press, 1959).

12. John Demos, "Notes on Life in Plymouth Colony," *William and Mary Quarterly*, XII, No. 2 (April, 1965), 266–267.

13. E. Franklin Frazier, *The Negro in the United States*, rev. ed. (New York: Macmillan, 1957), p. 368.

14. See John A. Hostetler, *Amish Society* (Baltimore: Johns Hopkins, 1963), pp. 162–164.

15. Clark Tibbitts (ed.), *Handbook of Social Gerontology* (Chicago: University of Chicago Press, 1960), p. 64.

16. Simmons, *op. cit.*, p. 33.

17. *Ibid.*, pp. 47–48.

18. William Graham Sumner, *Folkways* (Boston: Ginn, 1940), p. 280.

19. Simmons, *op. cit.*, pp. 177–216.

20. *Ibid.*, p. 228.

21. Tibbitts, *op. cit.*, p. 66.

22. *Ibid.*, p. 95.

23. *Ibid.*, p. 119.

CHAPTER FIVE

1. Ernest W. Burgess (ed.), *Aging in Western Societies: A Comparative Survey* (Chicago: University of Chicago Press, 1960), pp. 383–384.

2. For details concerning payments, source of funds, qualifying conditions, beneficiaries, and administrative organization in the United Kingdom, see *Social Security Programs Around the World* (Washington, D.C.: Department of Health, Education, and Welfare, 1964), pp. 208–209.

3. *Britain, An Official Handbook* (London: HMSO, 1966), p. 9.

4. *Ibid.*

5. *Ibid.*, p. 11.

6. *Ibid.*, p. 18.

7. *Ibid.*, p. 129.

8. For further details concerning treatment of the aged in Great Britain, see *Observation on the Care of the Aging in Europe* (87th Cong., 1st sess., House Committee Print No. 152, pp. 4–58 [Washington, D.C.: Committee on Veterans' Affairs, 1961]).

9. See *Homes for the Aged in Sweden* (Washington, D.C.: President's Council on Aging, 1962).

10. Burgess, *op. cit.*, p. 307.

11. *Ibid.*, pp. 304–311.

12. Alvin L. Schorr, *Social Security and Social Services in France*, Social Security Administration, Division of Research and Statistics, Research Report No. 7, p. 3 (Washington, D.C.: U.S. Department of Health, Education, and Welfare, 1965).

13. *Ibid.*, p. 4.

14. Ernest Burgess, *op. cit.*, p. 277.

15. See Marvin Sussman and Lee Burchinal, "Kin Family Network: Unheralded Structure in Current Conceptualizations of Family Functioning," *Marriage and Family Living*, XXIV, No. 3 (August, 1962), 231–240.

16. See Milton L. Barron, *The Aging American: An Introduction to Social Gerontology and Geriatrics* (New York: Crowell, 1961), pp. 55–68.

CHAPTER SIX

1. Sidney and Alice Pressey, "Two Insiders' Searchings for Best Life in Old Age," *The Gerontologist*, VI, No. 1 (March, 1966), 64.

2. Robert Havighurst, "Viewpoint, How Does It Feel to Grow Old?" *The Gerontologist*, VI, No. 3 (September, 1966), 130.

3. *The Older American* (Washington, D.C.: President's Council on Aging, 1963), p. 1.

4. *Ibid.*

5. Adopted from *On Growing Older* (Washington, D.C.: President's Council on Aging, 1964), pp. 19–36.

6. See also *Binocular Visual Acuity of Adults, United States, 1960–1962* (Washington, D.C.: Public Health Service Publication No. 1000, Series 11, No. 3, 1964).

7. See also *Hearing Levels of Adults by Age and Sex, United States, 1960–1962* (Washington, D.C.: Public Health Service Publication No. 1000, Series 11, No. 11, 1965).

8. See also *Selected Dental Findings in Adults, by Age, Race, and Sex, United States, 1960–1962* (Washington, D.C.: Public Health Service Publication No. 1000, Series 11, No. 7, 1965).

9. See also *Blood Pressure of Adults, by Age and Sex, United States, 1960–1962* (Washington, D.C.: Public Health Service Publication No. 1000, Series 11, No. 4, 1964).

10. See, for example, *Disability Days, United States, July, 1963–June, 1964* (Washington, D.C.: Public Health Service Publication No. 1000, Series 10, No. 24, 1965) and *Chronic Conditions and Activity Limitation, United States, July, 1961–June, 1963* (Washington, D.C.: Public Health Service Publication No. 1000, Series 10, No. 17, 1965).

11. Woodrow W. Morris, "Understanding the Aging Process: The Psychological Aspects," Supplement No. 9 to the University of Iowa bulletin *Adding Life to the Years*, XIII (September, 1966), 8.

12. *Ibid.*

13. For research up to 1960 on intelligence and problem solving among the aged, see Harold Jones in James E. Birren (ed.), *Handbook of Aging and the Individual* (Chicago: University of Chicago Press, 1959), pp. 700–738.

14. Dean Trembly and Johnson O'Connor, "Growth and Decline of Natural and Acquired Intellectual Characteristics," *Journal of Gerontology*, XXI, No. 1 (January, 1966), 9–12.

15. *Ibid.*, p. 10.

16. *Ibid.*, pp. 10–11.

17. *Ibid.*, p. 12.

18. James E. Birren, *The Psychology of Aging*, © 1964. By permission of Prentice-Hall, Inc., Englewood Cliffs, N.J., p. 162.

19. *Ibid.*, pp. 164–165.

20. *Ibid.*, p. 195.

21. For fuller details, see Ewald Busse, "Psychopathology," in Birren, *Handbook of Aging and the Individual*, *op. cit.*, pp. 364–399.

22. Morton Kramer, Earl S. Pollack, and Richard Redick, "Mental Disorders in the United States: Current Status and Future Goals," in Paul S. Hoch and Joseph Zubin (eds.), *Comparative Epidemiology of the Mental Disorders* (New York: Grune & Stratton, 1961), p. 80.

23. August B. Hollingshead and F. C. Redlich, *Social Class and Mental Illness* (New York: Wiley, 1958).

24. Forrest E. Linder, "The Health of the American People," *Scientific American*, CCXIV, No. 6 (June, 1966), 24.

25. *Ibid.*, p. 28.

26. *Ibid.*

27. Birren, *The Psychology of Aging*, *op. cit.*, p. 32.

28. See Staten W. Webster (ed.), *Knowing the Disadvantaged*, Part I of *The Disadvantaged Learner* (San Francisco: Chandler, 1966).

29. Birren, *Handbook of Aging and the Individual*, *op. cit.*, pp. 415–416.

30. See *Smoking and Health* (Washington, D.C.: Public Health Service Publication No. 1103, 1964).

31. See also *Mortality from Diseases Associated with Smoking, 1950–1964* (Washington, D.C.: National Center for Health Statistics, Series 20, No. 4, 1966).

32. *Mortality Trends in the United States, 1954–1963* (Washington,

D.C.: Public Health Service Publication No. 1000, Series 20, No. 2, 1966), pp. 50–53.

CHAPTER SEVEN

1. Wilbert E. Moore, *Man, Time, and Society* (New York: Wiley, 1963), p. v.

2. *Ibid.*, p. vi.

3. Michael A. Wallach and Leonard B. Green, "On Age and the Subjective Speed of Time," *Journal of Gerontology*, XVI, No. 1 (January, 1961), 71–74.

4. "Social Contribution by the Aging," in Clark Tibbitts (ed.), *The Annals of the American Academy of Political and Social Science*, CCLXXIX (January, 1952), 9.

5. See George P. Hunt, "Editor's Note," *Life*, September 23, 1966, p. 5.

6. Kathryn Powell and David Gover, "The Adolescent as a Consumer: Facts and Implications," *Marriage and Family Living*, XXV, No. 3 (August, 1963), 359–364.

7. *Ibid.*, pp. 360–361.

8. See Perry N. Priest, "Provision for the Aged Among the Sirionó Indians of Bolivia," *American Anthropologist*, LXVIII, No. 5 (October, 1966), 1245–1247.

9. Pauline Young, *The Pilgrims of Russian-Town* (Chicago: University of Chicago Press, 1932).

10. Bernard C. Rosen, *Adolescence and Religion* (Cambridge, Mass.: Schenkman, 1965).

11. Robert F. Spencer, Jesse D. Jennings, *et al.*, *The Native Americans* (New York: Harper & Row, 1965), p. 347.

12. Julian H. Steward and Louis C. Faron, *Native Peoples of South America* (New York: McGraw-Hill, 1959), pp. 365–367.

13. Monica Wilson, "Nyakyusa Age-Villages," *Journal of the Royal Anthropological Institute*, LXXIX (1949), 21–25.

14. See Robert Kleemeier (ed.), *Aging and Leisure: A Research Perspective in the Meaningful Use of Time* (New York: Wiley, 1961).

15. See Juanita Kreps (ed.), *Employment, Income, and Retirement of the Aged* (Durham, N.C.: Duke University Press, 1963).

16. See C. Wendall King, *Social Movements in the United States* (New York: Random House, 1965).

17. See Frederick S. Hulse, *The Human Species: An Introduction to Physical Anthropology* (New York: Random House, 1963).

18. Paraphrase from Wilbert Moore, "Aging and the Social System," cited in John C. McKinney and Frank T. De Vyver (eds.), *Aging and Social Policy*. Copyright © 1966 by Meredith Publishing Co. Pages 39–41 paraphrased by permission of Appleton-Century-Crofts, division of Meredith Publishing Co.

19. See Daniel Alleger, "Older People and Their Problems," *A Place to Live, The Yearbook of Agriculture 1963* (Washington, D.C.: U.S. Department of Agriculture, 1963), pp. 45–56.

20. See Helen Heusinkveld and Noverre Musson, *1001 Best Places to Live When You Retire* (Chicago: Dartnell, 1964).

21. For a popular article, see Bill Davidson, "Thistles in Paradise: The Truth About Retirement Housing," *Saturday Evening Post*, January 16, 1965, pp. 19–25.

22. See *Frauds and Deceptions Affecting the Elderly, Investigations, Findings, and Recommendations: 1964*, a report of the Subcommittee on Frauds and Misrepresentations Affecting the Elderly to the Special Committee on Aging, U.S. Senate (Washington, D.C.: U.S. Government Printing Office, 1965).

23. *Background Paper on Role and Training of Professional Personnel*, White House Conference on Aging, January 9–12, 1961 (May, 1960), Wilma Donahue, Chairman.

24. See, for example, *Aiding Older People: Programs and Resources in the Federal Government* (Washington, D.C.: Federal Council on Aging, 1958) and recent issues of *Aging* published by the Administration on Aging, U.S. Department of Health, Education, and Welfare.

CHAPTER EIGHT

1. See Ruth Albrecht, "The Meaning of Religion to Older People—The Social Aspect," in D. L. Scudder (ed.), *Organized Religion and the Older Person* (Gainesville: University of Florida Press, 1958), pp. 53–70; M. L. Barron, "The Role of Religion and Religious Institutions in Creating the Milieu of Older People," in Scudder, *op. cit.*, pp. 12–33; and Harold L. Orbach, "Aging and Religion: A Study of Church Attendance in the Detroit Metropolitan Area," *Geriatrics*, XVI (October, 1961), 530–540.

2. Edward G. Ludwig and Robert L. Eichhorn, "Age and Disillusionment: A Study of Value Changes Associated with Aging," *Journal of Gerontology*, XXII, No. 1 (January, 1967), 59–65.

3. See David O. Moberg, *The Church as a Social Institution* (Englewood Cliffs, N.J.: Prentice-Hall, 1962).

4. See Paul B. Maves, "Aging, Religion, and the Church," in Clark Tibbitts (ed.), *Handbook of Social Gerontology* (Chicago: University of Chicago Press, 1960), pp. 712–713.

5. Mollie Orshansky, "The Aged Negro and His Income," *Social Security Bulletin* (Washington, D.C.: Social Security Administration, U.S. Department of Health, Education, and Welfare, 1964), pp. 3–13.

6. *Ibid.*, p. 4.

7. Bureau of the Census, *Current Population Reports*, Series P–60, No. 41, October, 1963.

8. Orshansky, *op. cit.*, p. 6.

9. *Ibid.*

10. *Ibid.*
11. *Ibid.*, p. 3.
12. *Ibid.*, p. 12.
13. For an excellent study of the Townsend Movement, see Abraham Holtzman, *The Townsend Movement: A Political Study* (New York: Bookman, 1963).
14. For representative studies on this point, see Robert M. Dinkel, "Parent-Child Conflict in Minnesota Families," *American Sociological Review*, VIII, No. 4 (August, 1943), 412–419; James H. S. Bossard and Eleanor Stoker Boll, "Marital Unhappiness in the Life Cycle," *Marriage and Family Living*, XVII, No. 1 (February, 1955), 10–14; and Peter C. Pineo, "Disenchantment in the Later Years of Marriage," *Marriage and Family Living*, XXIII, No. 1 (February, 1961), 3–11
15. For representative studies see Ruth S. Cavan, "Family Life and Family Substitutes in Old Age," *American Sociological Review*, XIV, No. 1 (February, 1949), 71–83; Bernard R. Wrenn, "Three Generation Families: A Study of Three-Generation Family Units and Some Impacts on the Participants" (Master's thesis, Kent State University, 1954); Marvin R. Koller, "Studies of Three-Generation Households," *Marriage and Family Living*, XVI, No. 3 (August, 1954), 205–206; and William M. Smith, Jr., Joseph H. Britton, and Jean O. Britton, "Relationships with Three-Generation Families," the Pennsylvania State University, College of Home Economics Research Publication 155 (April, 1958).
16. See Paul H. Glasser and Lois N. Glasser, "Role Reversal and Conflict Between Aged Parents and Their Children," *Marriage and Family Living*, XXIV, No. 1 (February, 1962), 46–51.
17. See Irwin Deutscher, "The Quality of Postparental Life: Definitions of the Situation," *Marriage and Family Living*, XXVI, No. 1 (February, 1964), 52–59.
18. David and Vera Mace, *The Soviet Family* (Garden City, N.Y.: Doubleday, 1964), pp. 262–263.
19. Charles S. Cohen, "Research on Mental Abilities and Aging," *Adult Education*, XII (Spring, 1962), 171.
20. *Ibid.*
21. David O. Moberg, "Life Enrichment Educational Needs of Older People," *Adult Leadership*, XI, No. 6 (December, 1962), pp. 162–164, 185.
22. *Aging* (Washington, D.C.: Administration on Aging, January, 1966), No. 135, p. 3.
23. *Aging* (Washington, D.C.: Administration on Aging, February, 1966), No. 136, pp. 5–6.
24. *Aging* (Washington, D.C.: Administration on Aging, October, 1966), No. 144, p. 15.

CHAPTER NINE

1. For examples in sociology, see Pitirim A. Sorokin, *Fads and Foibles in Modern Sociology and Related Sciences* (Chicago: Regnery, 1956); C. Wright Mills, *The Sociological Imagination* (New York: Oxford University Press, 1959); Albert H. Hobbs, *The Claims of Sociology: A Critique of Textbooks* (Harrisburg, Pa.: Stackpole, 1951); and Maurice Stein and Arthur Vidich, *Sociology On Trial* (Englewood Cliffs, N.J.: Prentice-Hall, 1963).

2. For a well-written text, see Norman A. Polansky, *Social Work Research* (Chicago: University of Chicago Press, 1960).

3. The writer is indebted to Professor Rancel Hill, Department of Sociology and Anthropology, Kent State University, Kent, Ohio, for noting this distinction.

4. Carlos I. Reed, "Suggestions for Revision of Nomenclature on Aging," *The Gerontologist*, VI, No. 4 (December, 1966), 188–190.

5. *Ibid.*, p. 188.

6. *Ibid.*, p. 189.

7. *Ibid.*, p. 188.

8. Adapted from Gerald Gordon (ed.), "Research on Social-Psychological Aspects of Aging," *Progress in Health Services* (Chicago: Health Information Foundation, the University of Chicago, 1965), Vol. XIV, No. 2 (March–April, 1965).

9. *Ibid.*, p. 1.

10. *Ibid.*, p. 3.

11. *Ibid.*, pp. 4–5.

12. Hans L. Zetterberg, *On Theory and Verification in Sociology*, 3rd ed. (Totowa, N.J.: Bedminster Press, 1965), p. 63.

13. *Ibid.*, p. 64.

14. *Ibid.*, pp. 175–176.

15. Elaine Cumming and William E. Henry, *Growing Old* (New York: Basic Books, 1961).

16. Arnold M. Rose and Warren A. Peterson (eds.), *Older People and Their Social World* (Philadelphia: F. A. Davis, 1965), p. 360.

17. *Ibid.*, p. 361.

18. Robert Kastenbaum (ed.), *New Thoughts on Old Age* (New York: Springer, 1964), p. 4.

19. *Ibid.*

20. *Ibid.*, p. 5.

21. *Ibid.*, pp. 5–7.

22. Rose and Peterson, *op. cit.*, p. 362.

23. *Ibid.*, p. 363.

24. *Ibid.*, pp. 363–365.

25. *Ibid.*, pp. 3–16.

26. Abraham J. Heschel, "The Older Person and the Family in the

Perspective of Jewish Tradition," reprinted in *Aging* (Washington, D.C.: Administration on Aging, February, 1961), No. 76, pp. 10–13.

27. *Ibid.*, p. 10.

28. *Ibid.*, p. 11.

29. *Ibid.*, p. 12.

30. *Ibid.*, p. 13.

31. George A. Lundberg, *Can Science Save Us?* (New York: Longmans, Green, 1947).

32. *Ibid.*, p. 50.

33. *Ibid.*

34. In this connection, it might be useful to compare such publications as Nathan W. Shock (ed.), *Biological Aspects of Aging* (New York: Columbia University Press, 1962), and Ida Harper Simpson, John C. McKinney, *et al.* (eds.), *Social Aspects of Aging* (Durham, N.C.: Duke University Press, 1966).

INDEX